I0027173

LETS
GO
PUBLISH!

Tariffs Are
Good for America !!!

100 years ago America was completely funded by Tariffs. There was no income tax!

I wrote a book several years ago called Saving America. This book from the past offered a number of unique solutions to save America from economic ruin during the Obama era. At the time, we needed this book as Obama policies had brought our country to its lowest economic times. There were many problems and many solutions outlined in the book.

The problems magically began to go away when Donald Trump and Mike Pence knowingly or not, used the principles in this book to help bring America back. Even as good as America is doing today after miserable Obama years, the stubborn and corrupt mainstream media won't report the recovery honestly. Just this month the GDP is 4.1% DGP. The Obama legacy was that Americans had to get accustomed to growth below 2%.

Annual GDP growth never hit 3% in Obama's eight years, and economists have dubbed the Obama era as a "low growth." Period. Prior to the 2000's, the US was no stranger to annual GDP growth of 3%. In fact, conditions were so bad that there was an average annual GDP growth of just 1.48% during Obama's two terms. The press would have us believe that Obama began the recovery in his first year. Not so.

America has had more than one economic issue for sure, but it still is the best place to live on earth. When tackled one by one, all issues can be solved, and Donald Trump is solving them. This book shows the positive impact that Tariffs will have on solving the problems that prevent many people in American from living the dream. Donald Trump is completing his mission to make life better for all Americans

Just two years ago it was like all Americans were hunting for jobs. Too much government and too many industry-crippling regulations were a major source of the problem. Government was preventing the country from being successful. Government was blocking businesses from naturally solving their own problems; becoming successful and hiring lots of people. A good plan was needed to save US. The Trump team knew intrinsically that Tax and spend would not cut it. High taxes have been eliminated and the government is now more prudent as to how it spends taxpayer dollars.

During the Obama years, the country's issues included oppressive taxation; legal and illegal immigrants stealing the best jobs; regulations choking businesses; huge debt and deficits shackling our capital resources; a government healthcare system that added taxes and made health worse; and corporate offshoring which created a weaker nation. Additionally, we were victimized by having a massive energy dependency on our enemies. We were well on our way to socialism by redistributing wealth from producers to non-producers. Our prior administration permitted a huge, inefficient government to operate and to continually lie. It taxed too much and spent way more than it brought in. Under Obama, government became enemy # 1 of the people. A good plan, as shown in this book, was mostly implemented by Mr. Trump, and the results have been outstanding, though there are those with liar's disease who cannot see it right. A great leader named Donald J. Trump changed it all and along with Mike Pence, he saved US from an Obama perdition.

It has not been easy. Not only are Democrats and the corrupt press gunning for the President, but disgruntled RINOS as well as the leadership of the Republican Party are trying to minimize the results already on the table and those to come by this duly elected president. Now, our president is facing a Tariff war as he implements mercantilism to build up our manufacturing base and to correct the unfair trading that past presidents ignored. Those days are gone, and you will enjoy learning why Tariffs and mercantilism were good for America and the people and they still are. You won't want to put this book down.

BRIAN W. KELLY

Copyright © 2012, 2018 Brian W. Kelly   Publisher/ Editor, Brian P. Kelly
Tariffs Are Good for America!   Author, Brian W. Kelly
100 years ago America was completely funded by Tariffs. There was no income tax

All rights reserved: No part of this book may be reproduced or transmitted in any form, or by any means, electronic or mechanical, including photocopying, recording, scanning, faxing, or by any information storage and retrieval system, without permission from the publisher, LETS GO PUBLISH, in writing.

Disclaimer: Though judicious care was taken throughout the writing and the publication of this work that the information contained herein is accurate, there is no expressed or implied warranty that all information in this book is 100% correct. Therefore, neither LETS GO PUBLISH, nor the author accepts liability for any use of this work.

Trademarks: A number of products and names referenced in this book are trade names and trademarks of their respective companies.

Referenced Material: *The information in this book has been obtained through personal and third party observations, interviews, and copious research. Where unique information has been provided or extracted from other sources, those sources are acknowledged within the text of the book itself or at the end of the chapter in the Sources Section. Thus, there are no formal footnotes nor is there a bibliography section. Any picture that does not have a source was taken from various sites on the Internet with no credit attached. If resource owners would like credit in the next printing, please email publisher.*

Published by: .... LETS GO PUBLISH!
Publisher & Editor: ....Brian P. Kelly
Mail Location: .... P.O. Box 621, Wilkes-Barre, PA
Email: ....info@letsgopublish.com
Web site .... www.letsgopublish.com

Library of Congress Copyright Information Pending
Book Cover Design by Brian W. Kell,y Editing by Brian P. Kelly

ISBN Information: The International Standard Book Number (ISBN) is a unique machine-readable identification number, which marks any book unmistakably. The ISBN is the clear standard in the book industry. 159 countries and territories are officially ISBN members. The Official ISBN For this book is on the outside cover:

978-1-947402-53-9

The price for this work is :   **$9.95 USD**

10   9   8   7   6   5   4   3   2   1

Release Date: August   2018,

Dedication

I dedicate this book

To my wonderful brothers and sisters:

Angel Edward J. Kelly, Jr.

Nancy "Ann" Flannery

Mary A. Daniels

Joseph A. Kelly

I surely am a lucky person to have

Such wonderfulness in the family of

Edward J Kelly and Irene McKeown Kelly

.

Acknowledgments

I appreciate all the help that I have received in putting this book together as well as all of my other 164 other published books.

My printed acknowledgments had become so large that book readers "complained" about going through too many pages to get to page one of the text.

And, so to permit me more flexibility, I put my acknowledgment list online, and it continues to grow. Believe it or not, it once cost about a dollar more to print each book.

Thank you and God bless you all for your help.

Please check out www.letsgopublish.com to read the latest version of my heartfelt acknowledgments updated for this book. FYI, Wily Ky Eyely, my wonderful basketball playing "niece," loves this book and recommends it to all. She wants "Uncle Brian" to be our next US Senator.

Click the bottom of the Main menu to see the big acknowledgments!

Thank you all!

Table of Contents

Preface:

Why would anybody feel compelled to write a book about the benefits of Tariffs for America and Americans. Our country is not in imminent danger? Or is it?

Depending on how you define imminent, for eight years, we were in danger and we needed an innovative solution to bring us back on the right economic track. The idea was to have American businesses do so well that they could again put their "Apply Inside" signs back outside.

Donald Trump was the guy who began to make this all work the way he said he would during his campaign.

So, why did I write the original Saving America book during the Obama era. It is the book, upon which this book is based. Our economy had stopped working. Our financial institutions had been forced to lessen their standards while the taxpayer had become the prop between any of the government's favorite crony-backed businesses (including the banks) and failure. America was under attack from within and from without.

Government had one objective and that was to grow fast so that it could control everything and everybody. Corporations were protecting their assets and their viability from a government gone wild. The prior US government would seize whatever it could get from anybody and that includes corporations and their executives as well as the guy down the street.

The Obama government had great ambitions. Tax dollars are still the fuel that permits out-of-control government to grow and prosper and exercise all their leaders' ambitions. Our government wanted more and more and more from people who were making less and less and less while foreigners were taking their jobs. On the outside, we had free trade agreements nipping like piranha at all things American, while our own government accepted trade imbalance without a whimper and without a Tariff in reply.

Just two years ago it was like all Americans were hunting for jobs. Too much government and too many industry-crippling regulations were a major source of the problem. Government was preventing the country from being successful. Government was blocking businesses from naturally solving their own problems; becoming successful and hiring lots of people. A good plan was needed to save US.

The Trump team knew intrinsically that tax and spend program would not cut it. High taxes have already been eliminated and the government is now more prudent as to how it spends taxpayer dollars. You can see the results by the smiles on the people's faces when they cash their paychecks.

During the Obama years, the country's issues included oppressive taxation; legal and illegal immigrants stealing the best jobs; regulations choking businesses; huge debt and deficits shackling our capital resources; a government healthcare system that added taxes and made health worse; and corporate offshoring which created a weaker nation. US firms could make their goods offshore and then after stealing many American jobs, they paid no Tariff when they brought their goods back to America to sell. Unfair!

Additionally, the US was victimized by having a massive energy dependency on our enemies. We were well on our way to socialism by redistributing wealth from producers to non-producers. Our prior administration permitted a huge, inefficient government to operate and to continually lie. It taxed too much and spent way more than it brought in. Under Obama, government became enemy # 1 of the people.

A good plan, as shown in this book, was mostly implemented by Mr. Trump, and the results have been outstanding, though there are those with liar's disease who cannot see it right. A great leader named Donald J. Trump changed it all and along with Mike Pence, he saved US from an Obama and a second Clinton perdition.

President Trump was elected because he promised to say STOP. All of us together had to say STOP to save our country. We had to say STOP to save our lives. No matter who we were, it was time to STOP the government in its tracks. It was destroying us. We said STOP by electing Donald Trump and he put the brakes on the disaster we were encountering. s

What good would it have been even if our side—the side of right and justice won the game, if there were nothing left? America needed to come together, adopt a great plan to save the country and then fight for America and not for donor or lobbyist special interests. It was time for America to start winning again. And, so, we elected the most consistent winner of the ages as our new President in 2016, and he has already turned much of the malaise around

Donald Trump has already made America great again. Now, he is making America greater. Tariffs are one of his new tools to put the US ahead of our trading partners. Along the way, Trump has already just about saved America from the past eight years.

I had a plan back in 2012 when I first ran for the US Senate as a write-in candidate. I am running again by the way in Pennsylvania against Democrat Bob Casey Jr. in the fall election. From his actions, I can see that Mr. Trump was 100% in favor of that plan which like the Herman Cain "999"plan had three simple identifying letters, "RRR." How can anybody go wrong with a list of Rs such as this:

Reduce taxes; Reduce immigration; Reduce regulations; Reduce spending; Repeal Obamacare; Reindustrialize America; Reduce offshoring; Raise Tariffs; Revitalize energy; Reduce redistribution;

Reduce & eliminate lying; Reduce government; and Remember our mistakes. See how quickly three R's can become thirteen.

Once Trump was elected, the problems Americans were facing magically began to disappear as Donald Trump and Mike Pence, knowingly or not, used the principles in this book and its predecessors to help bring America back.

Even as good as America is doing today after the miserable Obama years, the stubborn and corrupt mainstream media still will not report the recovery honestly. They can't stand the truth. Just this month, the second Q 2018 GDP is 4.1%. That is amazing. Obama never once in eight years had a GDP in a quarter that equaled 3%. Despite the press squawking about the Trump Tariffs, the GDP went way up; not down as predicted by the corrupt media.

What boosted growth? The last Friday in July, the Commerce Department showed consumer spending rose by 4% in the second quarter, up from the 0.5% rate seen in the previous three months. Exports also grew by more than 9%, the fastest rate since the fourth quarter of 2013.

Some economists who think the glass is half empty noted that figure, which contributed more than 1% to the GDP gains, was inflated in part by farmers seeking to get ahead of new trade Tariffs on items such as soybeans. So, the Tariffs are having an effect.

As we know, in July, the US and China imposed Tariffs on $34bn of the other country's goods. Canada, Mexico and the European Union also imposed new duties in recent weeks on some US exports in retaliation for US Tariffs on steel and aluminum. Nonetheless, the US economy is booming.

Though Obama attempts to suggest his administration is responsible for the positive numbers, economists by and large do not agree. We all remember the Obama legacy. Everything was negative and the former President preached to Americans that US growth would never again get as high as even 2%.

Citizens had to believe that the Obama economic times were the best we would see in our lifetimes. The best the economy would do would be push growth above 1%. Now, he should get credit for 4.1% growth over a year and a half after his departure. I don't think so.

Whether Americans knew the cause or not, we felt it. Annual GDP growth never hit 3% in Obama's eight years, and economists thus dubbed the Obama era as a "low growth" Period. Prior to the 2000's, the US was no stranger to annual GDP growth of 3%. In fact, conditions were so bad before Trump that there was an average annual GDP growth of just 1.48% during Obama's two terms. The press would have us believe that Obama began the recovery in his first year. Not so. They do lie and very frequently. Trump calls their reporting "fake news."

America has had more than one economic issue for sure, but it still is the best place to live on earth. When tackled one by one, Donald Trump knew that all issues can be solved, and Trump is now in the process of solving them. This book shows the positive impact that Tariffs have had and will have on solving a number of the remaining trading problems that prevent many people in American from living the dream. Donald Trump is completing his mission to make life better for all Americans

I sure hope you enjoy this book and I hope that it inspires you to take action. I hope it helps you look at things differently. For example— corporations, unions, government, taxes, spending, and immigration need to be reined in.

A return to mercantilism and a whole host of other innovative items as defined by Donald Trump and by the R-R-R plan from a book down the road from the past, can help America survive this major economic slowdown before it melts our country. I hope you digest the entire plan, be willing to adopt it, and add to it your own positive notions. Tariffs are good for America and Americans.

Together, we can help make the US a far better country. First of course, we must make the most of having elected Donald Trump as our president. We cannot let RINO Republicans and slippery Democrats destroy America's opportunity for sustained greatness before we fully realize all the benefits. We have to throw the bums who slow Trump down out of office. Send them home.

Nothing worth having in life is easy. It has not been easy in the past two years, but the results are outstanding despite the fact that even Trump's allies, the Republicans have been fighting him. This must be stopped. Yes, not only are Democrats and the corrupt press gunning for the President, but disgruntled RINOS such as the Bushes and the Rubio's and others as well as the top leaders of the Republican Party have spent the last two years trying to minimize the results already on the table and they are trying to prevent the sure things that would come our way if they let our duly elected president execute his plan.

Now, our president is facing a Tariff war as he implements mercantilism to build up our manufacturing base and to correct the unfair trading that past presidents ignored. Those days are gone. The media must be ignored. Their mission is to replace Trump in the next election unless they can lie enough to force an impeachment. They are bad and good Americans cannot pay attention to the corrupt press. You will enjoy learning why Tariffs and mercantilism were good for America in the 1700's and good for the people and you will learn that they still are. You won't want to put this book down.

Brian W. Kelly
Author

About the Author

Brian W. Kelly is a retired Assistant Professor in the Business Information Technology (BIT) program at Marywood University, where he also served as the IBM i and midrange systems technical advisor to the IT faculty. Kelly developed and taught many college and professional courses in the IT and business areas. He is also a contributing technical editor to IT Jungle's "The Four Hundred" and "Four Hundred Guru" Newsletters.

A former IBM Senior Systems Engineer, he has an active consultancy in the information technology field, (www.kellyconsulting.com). He is the author of seventy-two books and hundreds of articles about IT and patriotic topics. Kelly is a frequent speaker at US events such as COMMON, IBM conferences, and other technical conferences and user group meetings across the United States. Brian has also accepted invitations to speak at political rallies on behalf of conservative and populist candidates.

Brian ran for Congress in 2010 in Pennsylvania and is currently running for the US Senate as a write-in candidate.

Chapter 1 Misguided US Economic Policies

A bad economy is a recent phenomenon

In the Preface, I posited this important question: "Why would anybody feel compelled to write a book about Saving America? From what? From whom? Is our country in imminent danger?"

I answered it quickly by saying "Depending on how you define imminent, we are in danger and we need a solution to bring us back on the right economic track so that American businesses can begin to do so well that they put the 'Apply Inside' signs back outside."

When Donald Trump became President because his love is for America and not for himself, he began by eliminating regulations to help get our economy back on track. Among many other notions, it worked. The Trump plan is very similar to the Saving America R-R-R Plan. It includes the following:

- Remove unnecessary regulations
- Close Tax loopholes
- Reduce taxes
- Make economy dynamic
- Bring back jobs from China & Mexico
- Pay attention to the debt limit
- Grow the economy at 6% annually by ending inversions
- Cut major unnecessary expenses
- Start cutting by eliminating the entire EPA & the Dept. of Education
- Secure a 35% boost to economy by eliminating the national debt
- Bring back steel and coal jobs
- Take advantage of US energy resources
- Eliminate & Replace Economically Unsound Obamacare.
- Etc. Etc. Etc.

Economic problems did not show up overnight

The solutions so far have had a major impact but nothing good happens overnight. However, now that we have changed direction, you will be able to smell the victory over the economy in the air. Without great leadership—the kind that has come from the Donald Trump Administration—America would still be getting both barrels from a dead Obama economy laden with misguided economic policies. They began in the last two years of the Bush Administration and have carried right through to Trump's inauguration. We had been in a ten-year funk.

You may recall that the Republicans lost control of Congress because Bush was perceived by the majority of Democrats to be ineffective against the ills of the day. And, so, the Democrats, two years before Obama became President, swept both houses of Congress and made George Bush a sitting lame duck President.

At the time, Americans, urged on by a corrupt fake news media, felt compelled to kick out the Republican Congress even though unemployment was low at 4.6 % and the debt was less than ten trillion. By the time that the Pelosi led House (They were in charge of the dollars) finished its two years and Bush was on his last Air Force One ride back to Crawford, Texas, unemployment was at 7.3%. The National Debt was over ten trillion dollars and when Obama became President it began its trajectory to just about $twenty trillion. Obama had raised the debt 7.917 Trillion. Unprecedented.

On the way to today, during the Obama Presidency, the unemployment rate went over 11% and the doctored rate tapered off for about a year to just over 8% and now with Trump in office it hovers around 4%.

During the Obama presidency, his experts in the Department of Labor figured out a way to not count those unemployed longer than six months in his unemployment statistics. They were still unemployed, but they did not count. This was done so the president would be able to brag about his fudged numbers to an unwary and for a long time, an adoring public.

Nonetheless, things were not good in the USA as more people were out of work than ever before. It felt bad and it was bad but it was reported by the corrupt press as being fine—nothing to worry about. When Obama left office, the debt was about twenty trillion and it was climbing fast with no end in sight.

However, things have definitely changed. Donald Trump is now the brightest light on the scene with a major promise to make America great again and now that he is getting that job done, his eyes are set on making America greater again. It was up to the voters such as you and I to give him the opportunity to help us and we did. He's up again in two years and we must remember how bad it was with the Democrats in power.

They say when your neighbor is out of work, it is a recession and when you are out of work it is a depression. During the Obama years, I was out of a job and a number of my neighbors were out jobs. I was fired by the University where I taught when I ran for Congress against a Democrat incumbent who had sent a lot of taxpayer dollars to the institution. After top-level evaluations as a professor at the university for years, I was replaced by a foreigner on a Visa from the University of Egypt. No kidding.

My one neighbor had a great job with the city but a new Mayor ended it for him. There are other stories out there but the job losses were very real. I know. My neighbors know. Many Americans know. Even low-paying Call Center jobs locally had about fifty applicants for each job. Let's just say that things were not good and it had been almost ten years since anything good has happened positively in our economy before Trump changed it all. Even my books are selling now.

So, while sitting in my man cave, thinking through the kind of things people in man caves think about; my first thoughts were about what could have made it so bad for Americans. After I had mulled that for a while, I spent a lot more time figuring out how to solve the problem by putting a great plan into the hands of a great leader. I have solved the problem on paper. You now have that paper in your hands right now in paperback or e-Book form. Thank you for your confidence. The Tariffs have a lot to do with the success.

If the Tariff notions outlined in this book are implemented as described, and the Democrats and never-Trumpers do not get to stop the tariffs now that they are having an impact, our economic problems will be solved, and they will be solved very quickly.

In 2012, when I initially wrote the Saving America book, nobody in government had the guts to implement this plan even though they knew it would work. Donald Trump is a different kind of leader... Finally! A lot of us are using prayer and we have our fingers crossed as a backup and we are pleased as punch that Mr. Trump now lives on Pennsylvania Avenue. Finally, a good American is making great decisions in the Oval Office, and the press is kicking and screaming every time he does something for the people.

So, let's ask ourselves what US economic problems are there that are so compelling that I would feel the need to devise a solution for them and then write a book about the solution so that others can see that the problems, though complex, are all solvable?

Therefore, before we explore solutions, we will take a broad brush look at what has been haunting the US and why before Trump, the economy was at the bottom level and why there were no good jobs left for regular Americans in the private sector.

Let me offer the quick answer first as to why.

The reason there were no real jobs to speak about other than those that on the average have cut the American middle class average wage by $5,000.00 in the last five years is simple to answer. The answer is: "The economy was bad and government officials did nothing." Yes it is obvious but that is not a joke.

Why was the economy so bad for almost eight years of President Obama's regime, which supposedly had been trying to make it better? This is a one word answer: "government." This is one of those times that if there were no government, things would have gotten better by themselves. Said differently "this is one of those times that if there were no Barack Hussein Obama ostensibly trying to make things better, things would have gotten better by themselves.

There have been lots of specific issues that caused America to be in a state of economic malaise. Let me talk about a few of them before we move on to the solutions in this about why Tariffs are a good thing.

Well, if you have been fortunate enough to have a job, you know that there are oppressive taxes that stifled individual, national, and business creativity. If you are a business owner, you were frustrated because whenever you peeked your head out of the company looking for a solution, the government played a game of whack-a-mole with your head. After licking your wounds, you would pick yourself up and try again but the prospects of your success with this regime were not very hopeful.

If you are a college graduate or you have an MBA or PhD, you may have found that just like me, legal and illegal immigrants were being hired before you for the few skilled jobs available. If you are a high school grad or a working mom without college skills, you may have found that Americans need not apply.

Small businesses have found government-created sustenance-choking business regulations that put them on a cliff riding a teeter totter—not sure about which way the wind would blow. People were finding more and more personal liberty & freedom being stolen by the government and though I do not understand it, there are still many who would not blame the Obama administration. Their love affair with President Obama endured while they used their access cards for food and necessities.

The government was spending money from China creating major deficits and adding to a huge national debt that has put the United States on the brink of bankruptcy. If the US were not the most successful country on earth, the other nations may have voted us out and asked for their loans to be repaid immediately. When running for office, Donald Trump predicted that if our debt reached $24 Trillion, we would be toast! Right now, we are at $21 Trillion and we had been climbing at a cool $Trillion per year under Obama.

And, yes, the big healthcare takeover added huge taxes, a big burden on businesses and the individual mandate socked regular people, especially the young. The people still pay more for health insurance than ever before in their lives.

Trump has been trying but he cannot get the Democrats and RINO Republicans to repeal the regressive Obamacare regulations even though we all know that from the beginning, Obamacare was a lie. Its intention was not better health care. It was to give government more control over the people. Over 1/6 of the economy has to do with health care, and government was able to gain full control.

It is getting worse before it gets batter

Plus as most already know there is no attempt to limit spending. There is more government spending than ever and the experts say for all that, our health and our healthcare has gotten worse. Meanwhile the crony friends of government officials are making millions from our misery.

You may know that under Obama, the US was reclassified as a de-industrialized (i.e. weaker) nation because most of our manufacturing is done overseas. That is another reason why Tariffs are good for America and Americans.

Offshoring has stolen the best American jobs and other than Trump nobody ever showed up on the political scene who knows how to bring them back. Worse than that, nobody in government was trying. In his nomination acceptance speech, Donald Trump promised that those days are over. America First! Watch what Mr. Trump does with Tariffs and please remember that no solution happens over night. A manufacturing plant cannot be built in a month.

But, with time, shuttered and almost finished plants can be brought back to life. For example, U..S. Steel Corp. is coming back and they credit Trump's Steel Tariffs. They plan to restart the second of two shuttered blast furnaces at their Granite City mill and they will hire 300 employees.

This is more good news after older good news from a March announcement that the Company would restart its other blast furnace at the Granite City Works in the Metro East and recall 500 workers. Steel was all but dead in the US. U.S. Steel had laid off hundreds of workers when it idled both furnaces in late 2015, with employment at the nearly 2,000 worker plant dipping as low as 100 in the ensuing two years.

The company has already begun to restart the first furnace and the second furnace should be in operation around Oct. 1, 2018. After the two restarts are complete, about 1,500 people will work at the plant, U.S. Steel says. Somehow the Trump Tariffs have already found success. Try to get someone from the press or the Democratic Party to acknowledge that.

"We are excited to announce that after the restart of the 'A' blast furnace on or around Oct. 1, all of the steelmaking operations at Granite City will be back on line, helping us meet an increased demand for American-made steel that has only grown since our March announcement," U.S. Steel President and CEO David Burritt said in a statement. "After careful consideration of market conditions and customer demand ... the restart of the two blast furnaces at Granite City Works will allow us to serve our customers' growing demand for high quality products melted and poured in the United States." Isn't that great news?

The first newly made steel in over two years came out of the plant very recently said Tom Ryan, an official with United Steelworkers Local 1899. He said the plant is close to hiring the 500 people U.S. Steel said it would hire in March. Many of them are experienced workers who have been waiting for years for the plant to restart, but Ryan said some former employees moved on during the long outage. "Everybody who was out there waiting for recall has been recalled," he said. "We're hiring off the street now and working diligently to do that." This is the new Trump economy. Bravo!

The plant never totally idled but it was close as US manufacturers found foreign sourced steel. From March 2017 to March 2018, over 700 workers were employed at the plant, according to Granite City Economic Development Director James Amos.

Things just don't happen. They are caused and this was all because of President Trump. The blast furnace announcements follow President Donald Trump's moves to impose Tariffs on all imported steel and aluminum this year. The Commerce Department in 2016 had slapped duties on imported steel from some countries, including China, Italy and other Asian nations after complaints they were selling steel at below-market prices. Trump announced in February a 25 percent Tariff on all imported steel. Bravo President Trump.

Tariffs will help the US bring back its manufacturing base. Trump has already said that the U.S. allies of Canada, the European Union and Mexico would no longer be exempted from the Tariffs. Of course these countries that were taking advantage of dumb government policies were very angry that their gravy train was coming to an end. The allies countered with threats of retaliatory Tariffs. The US is too big to fail and will not fail. Trump knows that and you and I know that.

Americans all see the closed plants

We all know that American Corporations left town over the last thirty years to make their products where wages were theoretically cheaper and taxes were lower. They come back often, however, to sell their products. They build their wares offshore and they bring those products back to America and pay no tribute to our country for the right to do business here. Donald Trump is pro American and he will not stand for this.

When they left town, they paid nothing to the US for the trauma they caused in moving the jobs offshore. They have left and during both Obama terms. They continued to leave whole towns unemployed. Regarding a Tariff war to stop American companies from Abandoning America, I say, "Bring it on."

Yet, big companies have gotten away with their plunder of Americans. I would call it big government corruption. They pay no unemployment compensation expense for their callous actions. America is left without the jobs and then American taxpayers must pay the unemployment claims of those left behind. Meanwhile, the establishment and corporate fat cats make more money and show their middle fingers to America. When they complain about Trump helping you and other Americans, quietly and discretely present them with your own home grown American finger.

Though we have tons of energy resources right here in this country and on our shores, until Trump was elected, our government insisted that we keep doing business with dirty, nasty, unfriendly enemies of the US rather than drill here and now. Hillary and Obama both vowed to put the coal mines in the US out of business while China was energizing its economy on coal and their economy began doing better than ours. Under Trump, the coal mines and natural gas fracking for energy is at record levels. The US is now an energy exporter. Amazing after just a year and a half of Trump with Democrats and Never Trumpers fighting his every move. i.

Our government had been more interested in splitting up a pie that wage-earners provide and giving a big share of that pie to non-wage earners. They could not understand that the right way is to stoke the economy to create a much larger pie simply by using sound economic principles designed to work. Donald Trump, an accomplished businessman knows this was a recipe for disaster and he is already changing everything to benefit America and Americans first. He is fixing the US underpinnings to make America great again!

The prior administration however, wanted the takers in our economy to depend more on government and vote for the Party that gave them their last free dollar. The truth is that for those Americans on the take, the state of the economy does not seem to matter to them. They get paid by the government. Work opportunities do not matter. They get their cash and sustenance from the government.

They don't feel very good about themselves as unproductive members of society; but our federal government trained them to suck it in and believe that it is better to feel worthless and depressed and have their access card than to have a nice paying job with five times earnings and a smile for the renewed opportunities and successes in life.

Government before Trump would feed this unwary population with propaganda so that those people would simply accept government as a master. Paying these people to do nothing is a big drain on our economy and it results in higher taxes for all of us. The prior government also seemed to enjoy lying to its citizens much more than telling the truth.

Government has become massive and dysfunctional. Without a proud American like Donald Trump and his judicious use of Tariffs, it would line up against the people. Yet, somehow, no matter how many times these leaders of just two years ago would mess up, they were willing to make the same mistakes again because a Luddite following would l re-elect them anyway. No more! The majority of the people have smartened up.

We all know with Trump that we can and will do a lot better than this. After Trump's acceptance speech, I am now convinced that the sky is the limit. What we need is a continuing of Trump's brand of "unique," plan for economic recovery and job creation with no BS like the prior eight years gave us. We now have a Trump plan that puts Americans first in all ways.

We need to make it even better as the nation straightens out the tax mess but also reaches into critical areas that are impeding economic growth today such as regulations, immigration, and excessive taxation and excessive spending. In the past eighteen months, the President has made much progress but there is more to be done.

For example, we need a plan that alters our pure capitalism system into one that adds more mercantilism. This will use Tariffs as in the turn of the century to help capitalism be even more successful. Mercantilism once provided the economic engine for the country when the founders were in charge and before the Wilson personal income tax.

Jobs are hard to come by anywhere in the world today except the United States. Since Trump was inaugurated over 3.2 million jobs have been created. Americans are still not used to the fact that jobs are available There are reports that jobs are becoming available so quickly that there are not enough people to fill them. We'll see.

During the Obama years, despite there being no jobs for anybody else, the number of US government employees was growing at a blinding speed. Federal and state employees were gaining jobs at a record pace. This is not part of anybody's economic solution. This is a big part of the problem.

Donald Trump has slowly but surely been addressing the glut in the federal workforce. For example, the federal government cut 3,000 jobs in May and federal employment has now dropped by 24,000 since President Donald Trump took office, according to data released today by the US Bureau of Labor Statistics. Even as federal government jobs were declining, the trump economy was causing overall employment to increase—as was employment in state and local government.

Most Americans know that when government grows, there is less and less real work even for government workers. And, so many agencies, even those that originally did good work in their functionary role as well as their advisory role to the President and Congress, have branched into areas that now hurt the economy rather than help it. The more government employees (other than the military) that are collecting paychecks, the greater the drag on private sector jobs and the economy as a whole. We can do lots better!

Why did I write this book?

Let me take another cut at why I wrote this book. President Trump is taking it on the chin everywhere you look for his Tariff plans, yet they are already helping American workers and most American businesses. There is no perfect fix to every problem.

Anybody paying attention knows that the Obama economy had stopped working. Some may have forgotten the tough times, especially if they had a nice government job. Our financial institutions have been forced to lessen their standards while the taxpayer has become the prop between any of government's favorite crony-backed businesses (including the banks) and failure. The United States once represented rugged individualism in all we did and only the strong survived. Now the weak are propped up by the strong. It's like having more than one family to support.

America became the strongest of nations because of the philosophy of rugged individualism. If you could not make it on your own, you had to hunt or fish or figure something out in order to survive. Joe was not permitted to take Mike's car or house or his full refrigerator just because Joe's was empty. Obama tried to change that but Trump is bringing it back.

Our government for the longest of times seemed like it was against strength as it attempted, through socialistic, progressive, and Marxist principles to create a society of wimps, in which the American dream was little more than a government handout.

Thank you President Trump for taking our side.

Chapter 2   From "9-9-9" to "R-R-R" With Love

Who would not want America to be saved?

As a conservative Democrat, I have gotten accustomed to saying things my Party does not like to hear. Quite frankly, I don't like what my Party says most of the time. I have begun to look to the GOP (non-RINOS, non-elites, non-establishment, and non-wimps) for the better ideas. Donald Trump has been delivering on what for years the GOP had promised.

Before Trump, in recent years, unfortunately, I have found that there are establishment elite Republicans and conservative Republicans. One is selfish and concerned only about advancing their individual causes, while the other is pro-American for the good of all Americans. It was shown time and time again in the Republican Primaries as the whining establishment could not stand how well conservative Cruz and conservative nationalist Trump were doing with the people. Thank you Mr. Cruz and Mr. Trump for knocking the socks off the establishment candidates.

Now that Trump has whooped Hillary for the presidency, I did think that Democrats might see the error of their ways and once again would become the Party of the people instead of the Party of radicals and those living off-the-wall. Therefore, I keep my "D" registration and I try to help the country. But I watch carefully because a new batch of RINO Republicans called Never-Trumpers joined the Democrats to attempt to undo the will of the people. They created phony crises such as Russian Collusion as it burns them that they are no longer in power. They are all sore losers.

My preference would be if the conservatives dropped the Republican Party and formed the American Party or the John Doe Party or something else. I'll bet a whole slew of old-time Democrats and

Independents would swarm to this new Party. That is not what this book is about, but I have spent time mulling over the notion in one of my recent books titled, *Kill the Republican Party*. That would be pretty easy for a frustrated Democrat to say, and the book was easy to write.

I created a plan which I called R-R-R in early 2012 in order to get beyond the rhetoric and to identify and solve the problems with our sour economy. In 2012 I wrote that "It is done and it will work whenever a leader emerges to adopt the thirteen simple principles of R-R-R." Donald Trump has already proven to be that leader.

Can you tell me why GDP, public debt, durable goods production, unemployment, the average wage, and many other economic indicators at the time of Trump's inauguration were at the worst levels since the Depression? As much as my father and your father liked Franklin Delano Roosevelt, he never brought the US to good economic times. But, like Obama, he sure talked a good story. Would it help us if we were to send the grave diggers out now so that we could ask Roosevelt to solve our economic dilemma?

I know I don't really think it would work if it were even possible. At least now we are only in the outer edges of a recession. With Roosevelt the country got the big banana—The Great Depression! But, to be sure that I was not on my own in my opinion of Obama's lack of accomplishments as a parallel to Roosevelt's in 2012, I reached out to the *New York Times*, and there it was in black and white from the most liberal newspaper in the world. This quote is from www.westernjournalism.com:

"The New York Times ran a featured story entitled, "Recession Officially Over, U.S. Incomes Kept Falling." The story highlights a study by two former Census Bureau officials, Gordon W. Green Jr. and John F. Coder, which found Americans have lost more wealth under the Obama administration than in the midst of the recession under George W. Bush. Altogether, the recession and Obama's policies created the largest reduction in the American standard of living in decades. Obama's policies have inflated store prices, debased the dollar's purchasing power, and led to a glut of unemployed who are not drawing a paycheck. However, government workers suffered the smallest income drop, meaning Obama's policies encourage government dependence and a further spiral toward economic catastrophe."

It had gotten so bad in the US, that I saw that we need a very serious, very creative, and very comprehensive solution to make it better. The R-R-R plan discussed briefly in Chapter 1 is exactly that. You may counter that all candidates from time immemorial have been trying to rescue poor economies, and create jobs, and they always think their ideas are the best. You would be correct. But, this time, the R-R-R plan with a lot of Trump moxie, looks like it will surely do it for us all. So, why is the R-R-R plan any better than same ole same ole? Let me digress first to the DNC's convention in Charlotte in early September, 2012.

You may recall that the Budget Buster in Chief in his 2012 Democratic National Convention speech, called for "the kind of bold, persistent experimentation that Franklin Roosevelt pursued during the only crisis worse than this one." Many bright Americans feared what Obama had in store for America in a second term that kept him in power until 2016. A number of experts reckoned that he gave it away at the convention.

So, for a time, there was rampant speculation that in the second term, Obama would re-create FDR's Works Progress Administration. It would have been part of what was supposed to be a massive government-funded jobs program. Obama never saw the budget, deficit and debt problem as worthy of being addressed because he saw his reelection as a mandate to ignore the debt and spend, spend, and spend and give people stuff. That's exactly what he did. There was no jobs program ever, and Obama never put forth a Works Progress Administration (WPA-like) plan. At least that would have been something.

Trump and Hillary 2016

Though Hillary has said numerous times that she endorsed Obama's economic policies when it came down to making her own mark, she was flexible and malleable enough to change her plan to whatever fit her needs. In the end, all elections come back to the economy—to jobs, wages, taxes, imports and exports, the price of goods and the cost of an education. Hillary and Donald Trump differed big-time on their plans to address these issues. Trump's ideas were more R-R-R capitalism and mercantilism, while Hillary was more socialist and communist, but not quite at the Bernie Sanders level.

From tax rates and immigration to globalization and the minimum wage, there were major contrasts between a potential Hillary presidency and a Donald Trump presidency. For one thing, Hillary's plan appeared to be warmed over Obama and the Trumps plan with R-R-R was a business oriented plan for success devised by a successful business entrepreneur. That's a big difference.

Regarding Jobs and incomes, Americans were understandably very anxious that the economy had not lived up to its promise over the past ten years of creating job growth that provides upward mobility and broadly shared prosperity. Instead, the nation went through what appears to be a continual recession marked by some bubbles in the stock market and in housing.

Trump won't settle for little dribbles. He predicted that he would and he now is creating the biggest economic boom in this country since the New Deal. As a businessman, he sees it as a no-brainer. He knows how to get it done. Trump has published his plans for large tax cuts and now installment one is a reality. He saw the viability of an economic surge and a jobs surge and he created it with his signature agenda items, particularly his push to limit immigration, to revisit trade agreements and to use Tariffs (mercantilism) to bring manufacturing back to America.

Hillary has unveiled a slew of policy dribble that all involved big-time government spending in excess of the budget busting job done by Obama. She was ready to provide everything from job training and free community college education to broadband networks, infrastructure, and clean energy. She had not considered how this all could be paid for. other than increasing the debt and deficit.

Mrs. Clinton backed Obama's efforts to raise the federal minimum wage, to overhaul immigration laws, and to boost women's workforce participation by backing efforts to improve paid leave and access to child care. The problem with Hillary's plans were that these items for the most part have been on Obama's plate for a long time and they have gotten stale from inaction. Why now? People rejected them. Where have they been? Where was the funding?

Though Bill Clinton and Barack Obama got us into the trade deal arena with their many bad deals, if you can believe Hillary, she said she and Donald Trump think the same on the new 12-nation Pacific trade deal, negotiated and promoted by the Obama administration. Hillary says she and Trump are also questioning the ages old North American Free Trade Agreement, or NAFTA, which her husband Bill Clinton pushed. How Hillary really felt on all that, thankfully we will never have to know.

Trump was and is unhappy with what he saw as Obama's political friends with his blessing having aggressively pursued a policy of globalization—moving our jobs, our wealth and our factories to Mexico and overseas. Though she denies it, Trump links Hillary to the 1994 NAFTA deal that her husband President Clinton signed, which has destroyed jobs in America. Trump got rid of it as soon as he could in his administration.

Trump has such strong opposition to trade deals that he has had open clashes with the U.S. Chamber of Commerce—the biggest business lobby. Trump is in favor of mercantilism as in the R-R-R plan to even the playing field for loyal US manufacturers who continue to employ American workers in America. Trump did not believe what Hillary said was true; nor did most Americans.

Trump wanted a nice big tax cut for all so that America can stimulate its success engine. It took a year but he finally got it with a lot of hard work. Mr. Trump slashed tax rates and pushed millions of households off the income tax rolls with a proposed tax cut that was nearly triple the size of the Bush tax cuts of 2001 and 2003. His real plan was that when they came off the income tax rolls, they would have a nice job and a nice income to get them back on the rolls at a better level. We have already experienced the Trump plan and American prosperity is returning.

FYI, R-R-R is not a warmed over "9-9-9" from Herman Cain. In fact, tax policy, the thrust of 9-9-9, though very important, is just one area of R-R-R's many facets. Along with a number of other features, R-R-R is built to move our economy from one that is pure Capitalism to a modified Capitalism / Mercantilism system. When in the Trump Plan, I heard Mr. Trump speak about solving the problem of

American Corporations abandoning America, he was talking about
R-R-R and Mercantilism without mentioning their name

Chapter 3 What is Mercantilism?

Mercantilism is in essence a propitious use of Tariffs to help the home country

Mercantilism is the method the founders enhanced and in fact, it is how the founders financed the government when they were in charge. Capitalism is a core element of an R-R-R style Mercantilism.

At economist.com, they discuss MERCANTILISM as one of the great "whipping boys" in the history of economics. The school of mercantilism, which dominated European thought between the 16th and 18th centuries, is now considered little more than a historical artefact. In other words, no self-respecting economist of today would describe themselves as mercantilist. I can say mercantilism 'Я US because I actually believe that it has some healing powers that Perhaps Donald J. Trump sees also.

Despite how today's economist may see it, the use of the mercantilist doctrine is one of the foundation stones of modern economics. Yet its dissipation has been less total than an introductory economics course might suggest.

What is the essence of mercantilism?

The ticking heart of mercantilism is the view that maximizing net exports is the best route to national prosperity. Mixed in there is some theories of Tariffs and some old ideas that the gold standard is all that matters in monetary policy. Some say that in essence mercantilism is "bullionism". Of course bullionism is the idea that the only true measure of a country's wealth and success is the amount of gold that it has. Thus, if country A had more gold than country B, it was by definition, better off.

These were not light principles when mercantilism guided countries into successful economics. This idea also had important consequences for economic policy. Picture the recently founded United States. Go back to 1492 and the 1600 period settlements and we know that America was alive and well. How could the US engage in trade with other countries while maintaining its own superiority. Back when, the best way of ensuring a country's prosperity was to make few imports and many exports. Better for foreigners to owe you than you them. The objective was to generate a net inflow of foreign exchange and maximizing the country's gold stocks while shipping products to the paying countries.

Such ideas were attractive to some governments. There were no such institutions as the federal reserve so gold was the standard and he who had the most gold was always the winner. Accumulating gold was thought to be necessary for a strong, powerful state. Countries such as Britain implemented policies which were designed to protect its traders and maximize income. So, there were two aspects. One is that there would be no gold inflow if the traders were outmuscled by foreign companies, so means needed to be developed that would keep the home country producers busy building products to export.

The Navigation Acts, which severely restricted the ability of other nations to trade between England and its colonies, were one such example. England became the most powerful nation on earth before the US because it depended on mercantilism and a huge national treasury.

The Economist people tell some amusing (and possibly apocryphal) stories of bullionism in action. During the Napoleonic Wars, the warring governments made few attempts to prevent their foes from importing food (and thereby starving them). But they did try to make it difficult for their opponent to export goods to build up their coffers to create armaments.

Fewer exports would supposedly result in economic chaos as gold supplies dwindled. Ensuring an absence of gold, rather than an absence of grub, was perceived to be the most devastating way to grind down the enemy. And, of course nobody had to see the painted images of starving people.

The Economist suggests that there is a huge and important distinction between mercantilist practice and mercantilist thought. The opinions of thinkers were often mangled when they were translated into policies. A paper by a gentleman named William Grampp, published in 1952, offered a subtler account of mercantilism. All of this is germane in 2018 as America still needs its supply of reserves to come into the world economy—gold or not.

Mr. Grampp offers that mercantilists were big on foreign trade. One often reads in mercantilist literature that foreign trade would be more beneficial than would domestic trade. And some of the early mercantilists, like John Hales, were enchanted by the idea of an overflowing treasure chest. FYI, Hales was an English public official and parliamentarian, who was one of the leading "Commonwealth" writers of Tudor England

But Mr. Grampp argued that, on the whole, the thinkers needed to stop confusing mercantilism with bullionism. Few mercantilists cared about the balance of payments. In fact, they were taken back by the idea that anybody would hoard gold and silver. This is because many mercantilist thinkers were most concerned with maximizing employment, which comes into play with mercantilism and not bullionism.

There was a man named Nicholas Barbon. He had pioneered the fire insurance industry after the Great Fire of London in 1666. He had a deep interest in money being invested and put to use, and not hoarded. As William Petty—arguably the first "proper" economist— argued, investment would help to improve labor productivity and increase employment. And almost all mercantilists considered ways of bringing more people into the labor force. In that the production of goods required workers, there was a symbiosis between mercantilism and bullionism on many fronts.

Mr. Grampp added a mercantilist twist to Keynesian economics suggesting that it "has an affinity to mercantilist doctrine", given their shared concern with full employment. Keynes, in a short note to his "General Theory", approvingly quotes mercantilists, noting that an ample supply of precious metals could be key in maintaining control over domestic interest rates, and therefore to ensuring adequate resource utilization.

Mercantilism is thought to have begun its intellectual eclipse with the publication of Adam Smith's "Wealth of Nations" in 1776. A simple interpretation of the economic history suggests that Smith's ruthless advocacy for free markets was squarely opposed to regulation-heavy mercantilist doctrine. But according to research by Lars Magnusson of Uppsala University, Smith's contribution did not represent such a sharp break.

The father of economics was certainly concerned with the effects of some mercantilist policies. He saw the damage that overweening government intervention could do. Smith argued that the East India Company, a quasi-governmental organization that managed parts of India at the time, was responsible for creating the huge famine in Bengal in 1770. And he hated monopolies, arguing that greedy barons could earn "wages or profit, greatly above their natural rate". Smith also grumbled that legislators could use mercantilist logic to justify stifling regulation.

But Smith points out circumstances in which government interference is necessary. He was in favor of the Navigation Acts (1651, 1660) For example, The Navigation Act of 1651, which was aimed primarily at the Dutch, required all trade between England and the colonies to be carried in English or colonial vessels, resulting in the Anglo-Dutch War in 1652.

In Smith's lesser-known "Lectures on Jurisprudence", he outlined other cases where government intervention in trade was useful. Smith was not opposed to regulation per se, but rather instances where individuals and governments could abuse their position of power for personal gain. We have seen this in our own country such as all the Obama cronies who received the stimulus money during the great recession.

Though most of the world's rich countries remain committed to free trade today, mercantilist themes are often found in economic policy debates. China and Germany are often envied for their trade surpluses or seen as economic models, and China especially has very deliberately subsidized exports. President Barack Obama made a doubling of American exports a major policy goal, as part of his plan to help America "win the future". However it did not happen as the Obama item du jour always took priority.

The overall zero-sum way of looking at the global economy is less rooted in the national greatness side of mercantilism than in the focus on full employment and the success of the home land.

Many rich economies for years, even the US economy has been suffering from insufficient demand and high rates of joblessness; it can be decreed a thoroughly Keynesian, in other words. Early in the US recovery some economists presented a shill of intellectual credibility to this perspective. Paul Krugman, for instance, who first consults popular liberal progressive thinking before he speaks wrote of America's 2010 trade agreement with South Korea as such:

> *There is a case for freer trade — it may make the world economy more efficient. But it does nothing to increase demand.*

> *And there's even an argument to the effect that increased trade reduces US employment in the current context; if the jobs we gain are higher value-added per worker, while those we lose are lower value-added, and spending stays the same, that means the same GDP but fewer jobs.*

> *If you want a trade policy that helps employment, it has to be a policy that induces other countries to run bigger deficits or smaller surpluses. A countervailing duty on Chinese exports would be job-creating; a deal with South Korea, not.*

Back to bullionism. The case for bullionism as a demand stimulus dissipated with a role for bullion in monetary policy. The introduction of fiat money meant that balance-of-payment goals were unnecessary to maintaining a particular monetary policy stance, since central banks no longer needed an adequate hoard of gold to pump money into the economy.

The mercantilist temptation is a strong one, however, especially when growth in the economic pie slows or stops altogether. More than two centuries after Smith's landmark work, economics' foundational debate continues to resonate.

Debate all you want, Mercantilism helped the US from its inception as an entity through becoming a country to the 1910-1920 era. Then with Wilson's baby, the Personal Income Tax, the government could grab all it wanted from corporations and from the people. Ironically, the taxpayers permitted the illegal income tax to become legal. Would you vote for a personal income tax today if you had a choice. The founders counted on Americans saying no forever to a Federal Income Tax. For those who do not like the founders, that fact alone ought to create a reevaluation.

Can I be a socialist or a progressive or a conservative and still find value in mercantilism?

The good news for conservatives is that Mercantilism does not resemble Progressivism, Marxism, Communism, or Socialism. We've had enough of that over the last eight years. Haven't we?

As a superset of Capitalism, Mercantilism is designed to first help the home country. (America First!) That country in our case is the USA! Mercantilism is often deployed when a country is in a fledgling status or when it has become disadvantaged. I would suggest that the latter describes US pretty well. The US is still king of the hill, but we are declining. The US is the place to be but those countries rushing the hill are increasing in number and unlike US, they do not have their hands tied behind their backs by their governments as in the Obama regime.

The Trump R-R-R plan is simply good for the economy, but it is not simple. It is good for the people, but it is not a handout. It is good for jobs, but it does not take tax money to pay workers such as $30,000.00 per year while costing taxpayers $200,000.00.

Those are Obama plans and Hillary Clinton's plans and they have been proven ineffective. Obama retired and then began a deep state organization to rid the planet of Trump, while Hillary was defeated but chose not to accept her defeat. If Obama's plans were going to work, they would have already worked and we would not be having this discussion right now, and Hillary would be President. Hillary should blame Obama's failure with economics for her own.

Corporations are not people, but they represent an awful lot of people. For those corporations that want to sign up to be American-

Centric, the R-R-R plan is good for corporations. It is a solution balm that offers a gutsy, unique, realistic, and workable path to getting America back on its feet. There is nothing like it anywhere else. All we need as a country is the resolve and the right leadership for the R-R-R plan to make us all successful. My perspective is that Donald Trump has become that leader.

Here are the four full sets of R-R-R

Set 1: Reduce Taxes; Reduce Immigration; Reduce Regulations
Set 2: Reduce Spending; Repeal Obamacare; Reindustrialize America
Set 3: Reduce Offshoring; Raise Tariffs; Revitalize Energy
Set 4: Reduce Redistribution; Reduce Lying; Reduce Government

There is even an extra R that we typically lump in with Set 4. It is *Remember Mistakes.* It may be the most important.

Please note that *The Thirteen R Plan* did not have the ring of *R-R-R,* and so we opted not to use it.

The principles of R-R-R Mercantilism were practiced in our founding and it guided the country through its formative years as America grew stronger and stronger. The country that taught the US how to run our economic affairs is England. Now, unfortunately, both of us have lost our ways:

Here is England's Mercantilism trade statement from 1549:

"We must always take heed that we buy no more from strangers than we sell them, for so should we impoverish ourselves and enrich them." With that the old England ruled the world until 1860 when this slogan was no longer its guiding light.

England abandoned Mercantilism and became intrigued with free trade. Both presidential candidates in 2012 and most of Congress were advocates of the same free trade notions that England toyed with and finally adopted for real. England abandoned the principles that had made her strong. The US, when it practiced mercantilism v free trade kicked England out of the marketplace and took over.

Hillary Clinton in 2016 was for the failed Obama trade deals of the past such as NAFTA and TPP, while Trump has already eliminated both of them. They were poorly negotiated deals that have been inflicted on America. Trump either gets out or renegotiates deals. He would prefer to walk away from the table rather than accept a status quo that hurts America. Hillary was ready to leave things as they were as long as she could be the queen.

Who else liked mercantilism?

In addition to the ever-strong United States, Germany was a great student of Mercantilism. Coincidentally just 10 years after England abandoned Mercantilism, Germany began to excel in steel manufacture, in textile work, in mining and trading, in every branch of modern industrial and commercial life, and also in population.

President Wilson in the early 1900's noted that "German development has been … amazing." Unfortunately, Wilson was not a Mercantilist. He was a progressive with little economic knowledge other than the power of high taxation. .

Abandoning Mercantilism almost cost England World War I. America, still practicing R-R-R Mercantilism, saved the day for the Brits. Germany was in the process of picking England apart in World War I, and was ready to succeed when US President Wilson agreed to help.

Germany had achieved its success by practicing mercantilism, which, of course they had learned from the mighty British—old England herself—and they had carefully watched the prosperity of the US increase with mercantilism while England declined. Our assistance to England in World War I helped ole England avoid becoming a German Isle.

By 1860, England lost its standing in the world as a commercial force when it abandoned Mercantilism. By 1920, President Wilson, a progressive ideologue, had begun to change the US from mercantilism to full capitalism with just a dose of socialism, his true advocacy, for good measure.

It took a long time. However, once the notion was in place it grew throughout the 20th century and into the 21st. The US eventually dropped mercantilism as our economic creed, and we adopted free trade as our national mantra. It was a big mistake. It took time but our economic power declined gradually. Finally, here we are with a debt that is now bigger than our total GNP. That is what happens when progressivism takes a big ride on the slippery slope.

Eventually England was flattened by her liberal free trade policies. mercantilism helped America overtake England as the greatest industrial power. England lost 50% of its economy moving from mercantilism to free trade. By 1944, the English pound officially lost its role as the reserve world currency. The US dollar took its place

Just like we beat England when we practiced mercantilism, unless we change back, the Chinese, strong advocates of protecting their home industries via mercantilism, will do to us what we did to England from 1860 onward. It doesn't happen overnight but China's ascendancy to become the most powerful nation in the world is well on its way. This will be China's success while it is America's shame. Shame on US! The good news in 2018 is that Donald Trump sees this but he must deal with the buffoons in Congress to get big measures done.

Like England, in 2016, Americans knew that unless we changed our top leadership to a man with the insights of Donald Trump, and we convinced our new leaders that R-R-R Mercantilism was the path to success, we would be remembered as a country that once had it all.

We could have chosen a course that helped America, rather than just helping America's largest corporations and third-world countries. Free trade and greed would have been listed as the major cause of our undoing. But, we voted Donald Trump, a businessman as our president.

China has been a major practitioner of mercantilism. They are prospering while others, who believe in free trade are declining. That is why our free traders lose every day to China in negotiations. Free trade is not good for America. Donald Trump preaches about how the Chinese whoop us in trade at every outing. Yet, every candidate for President in 2012 and 2016, other than Donald Trump, who needs a way to punish American Corporations gone offshore, is a proponent of free trade. That is exactly why our economy had been stinking up the world before Trump.

Pat Buchanan sums up free trade as follows:

> *"With the abolition of Tariffs, and with US guarantees that goods made in foreign countries would enter American free of charge, manufacturers began to shut plants here and more production abroad to countries where US wage-and-hour laws and health & environmental regulations did not apply, countries where there were no unions and workers' wages were below the US minimum wage. Competitors who stayed in America were undercut and run out of business, or forced to join the stampede abroad."*

The American people, with help from anti free trade advocates such as conservative Pat Buchanan can quash the notion that free trade is helpful to regular Americans. It is not. It is certainly helpful to CEOs of huge companies, but they do not need help from average Americans or from the government. Write your Congress and offer your thoughts on free trade. It surely is not free. It has a heavy cost.

I offered the R-R-R plan to all Republican candidates for President in 2012 and none of them took me up on it. I checked them all out and unfortunately, they are on Obama's side on free trade and this is very disappointing. Before he chose not to run, I hoped back then that Donald Trump was elected and that he would go back to his idea of fair trade and abandon free trade as it would have hastened our economic recovery. At least it would have forestalled our demise. My prayers were answered. Trump is now our President.

R-R-R Mercantilism is clearly not something that free traders like. The reason America lost all the time was why the economy was destined to stay in the toilet until we change the belief that America can lose in all trade agreements and still wind up a winner. Mr. Trump changed all that and boy I could not be happier. No matter how many 1000 dollar losses a gambler sustains without winning, when they hit a very large number, they do not win. Their losses are just bigger. Trump has made America a winner.

When Hillary and Bill Clinton, Al Gore, John Kerry, and Nancy Pelosi are for something, I want conservative leaders such as Donald Trump to be against it. So, far, before Trump just about all politicians from both Parties are for free trade. It is a bad idea for America. Trump is for FAIR trade. The old way was a collusion called bi-partisanship and it was killing America because nobody wanted to fix its biggest problem – getting whooped big time in free trade deals which put Americans out of work. Donald Trump knows what he is talking about.

Free trade has not been fair to US citizens as there were lots less jobs when Mr. Trump was inaugurated President. Our average wages had decreased by 10 to 12%. Let me repeat. Free trade is not good for America. It is good for every other country that wants to beat us in the world economy. R-R-R Mercantilism is the right plan for our future success. It is our opportunity to regain world leadership.

The R-R-R plan is more than just Mercantilism but unless the US can again own our own economy, instead of giving it away freely to every third world country, as well as China, the full benefits of R-R-R cannot be realized. Even so, there are enough other good points that R-R-R can still help America in many ways. We should all be very pleased that one of the few people in America who understands this is President Trump and he is already making life better for Americans.

If Trump were not our President. as the US weakened, economists were predicting that the Chinese *yuan*, aka *renminbi* would overtake the dollar in the next five or ten years as the world's reserve currency. This would be more than symbolic. It would be a direct reflection of poor leadership. I don't think we have to worry with Donald Trump, a smart man who loves America.

Earlier in 2012, then French President, Nicolas Sarkozy, who was hoping to be re-elected, but was not, fired a big shot at the failing Brits. He said Britain was a country with 'no industry.' I was worried that he would say that of US? I wondered if we could exist with no industry? Would China begin to manufacture our war materials? I wondered if we had a chance in the future without refocusing our attention to our real problems?

R-R-R Mercantilism is a philosophy designed to solve problems and answer many questions including: "How do we get back all the jobs exported in the last 30 years?" If we want to re-industrialize America, just like the Chinese, we have to protect our markets and support our domestic industries. It is that simple. The solution is called R-R-R. The solution provider is already in office and he is doing his best to overcome internal obstacles to make America great again.

R-R-R Mercantilism is the key to America's recovery. It is not just one of the R's, it is a combination of five major R's and to a lesser degree, all of the R's in the R-R-R program. Mercantilism is the one word short description for implementing at least these five R's: *Reduce Taxes, Reduce Regulations, Reindustrialize America, Reduce Offshoring,* and *Raise Tariffs*. Mercantilism is in fact, the very opposite of *"free trade."*

For those who are free trade advocates, as noted above, you can think of mercantilism as anathema to free trade. R-R-R Mercantilism places the interests of the people of the United States in front of all other interests, whether they are foreign or domestic. R-R-R Mercantilism provides a way for all domestic businesses to be successful but its real focus is to make people successful because businesses are successful. Today's capitalism permits businesses to be successful even if the people in the home country are jobless. Mercantilism corrects a big hole in that logic.

R-R-R Mercantilism rewards businesses that stay at home to produce goods here and provide high paying jobs here. It uses a big carrot to encourage businesses to think America-first! Likewise, it uses a big stick to discourage those companies that would take even more than the 20,000,000 manufacturing jobs already gone, to a foreign country. The objective is for companies to come back to America because it will be more profitable for them and it will be better for the American people. Thank you Donald Trump for not needing this book.

Chapter 4 Offshoring: Bad for American jobs

Analysts during the last years of the Obama administration have been suggesting that over the next decade or two American corporations plan to offshore as many as 40,000,000 additional jobs. It doesn't take much logic to see that would destroy the fabric of our country and eliminate most of the middle class. President Obama was able to declare the existence of a war on women and a war on the middle class, but he sure had no solution to what his policies have forced businesses to do. A country with no jobs is a lost country.

When and if the next 40,000,000 jobs got the call under Obama to be offshored, this time, the jobs that would be lost would be the best white collar jobs that exist—not hamburger flippers. These jobs would be—engineering jobs, accounting jobs, radiologist jobs, and other highly paid professional jobs. Technology will help the supposedly American companies destroy the US job market if we let them get away with it. Donald Trump is bigger than all technology firms thank God and he loves America.

Donald Trump will not let that happen. Trump has tweeted his disdain for offshoring and warned companies considering it.: He told companies considering offshoring that his plans would make leaving financially difficult, adding: Please be forewarned prior to making a very expensive mistake!

There are many things that appear to minimize the need for jobs but instead enhance the creation of better jobs. The computer, invented in the 1940's is pervasive on desktops in the mainframe room, in cars, and microwave ovens and it has impacted jobs in a positive way. Just because a device makes things easier does not mean that people will become obsolete in the workplace.

You may know that in the US today, we already have remotely controlled robots performing Telesurgery. Today a human surgeon is still required. Picture a surgeon in New York City operating on a patient in Los Angeles through robotic technology and high speed communications. In ten years, if R-R-R is taken off the table as a solution, and we do nothing, will the picture change? Will we see a surgeon in Shanghai operating on a patient in New York or Los Angeles? I think so. America must protect its jobs and Tariffs / mercantilism is one of the best ways to do so.

The warning is that American officials must stop the exporting of American jobs overseas. R-R-R mercantilism is the answer. It is designed to make America the go-to nation again! Go-to nations get the jobs. R-R-R and mercantilism are designed so that twenty years from now, America will not be known only as that country that provides raw materials to the manufacturing leader of the world—China.

Mercantilism is capitalism with the rounding factor in favor of the home country, not the corporation. In our case, of course, the home country is the United States of America. Mercantilism is one of the big cures for offshoring.

When you fly, they tell you in the event of cabin decompression, put your mask on first so you can take care of your children. The America economy before Trump's election was in decompression mode. As nice as it sounds, under the guise of "free trade," we cannot continue to be helping other countries get stronger than US, while we have had our masks yanked from our faces by our own government. Trump is ruffling a lot of feathers by proposing Tariffs on countries whose trade policies hurt the United States.

He knows it is time for Americans to put our own masks back on. Do not expect government to solve this for us. Now that we have a great change in our leadership, we can do anything. Besides a great President, which we now have, we need an America-first Congress to help us get that job done. Donald Trump is for America and Americans first!

R-R-R Tariffs and mercantilism are major components of our oxygen mask for both survival and great success. There will be no more decompression.

Chapter 5 Say No to the Status Quo!

A Plan for America & Americans 1st

How about this for a great Donald Trump mantra: "SAY NO TO
THE STATUS QUO!" This is another new mantra and a great
slogan for all Americans after we have endured eight years of Barack
Hussein Obama. With Mike Pence in the administration and with
Donald Trump in the driver's seat, after a strong nationalist / populist
showing in the 2016 elections, Americans have not had to worry
about the status quo messing with Americans after January 2017. We
do have to worry about the Democrat resistance and the Never
Trumpers who would like to teach Trump a lesson by hurting
America.

The plan Trump is executing to revitalize the economic has been
around for some time and it has been attacked by many Democrats as
would be expected. Democrats had eight years with no plan to
improve the economy. The Trump plan is full of good meat for
conservatives and it seems that even without the Never Trumpers and
the Democrats the President is having great success.

Since the "In-the-tank-for-Obama" corrupt US media does not like to
dig into anything well to do their jobs, all the banter against Trump
has been speculation and of course lies. There was a joke that before
my two sons became lawyers I used to tell all the time. What is the
difference between a dead skunk in the middle of the road and a dead
lawyer in the middle of the road. After a pause! There are skid marks
in front of the skunk.

The press is still in the tank for Obama as they are more interested in
securing the Obama legacy of a weak economy rather than help
America and Americans. With so many lies told by the press in their
daily fake news narrative, they are literally unbelievable. Substitute

the press for the lawyer and we still have skid marks in front of the skunk.

During the election period of 2016 as Hillary and a corrupt justice department were both fighting to not go to jail and fighting though tepidly to become president Hillary Clinton and her minions enjoyed making light of the Trump plan. The irony for Hillary and the Democrats of today is that they have no plan of their own other than *Barack Obama's Status Quo Plan* which I would subtitle *Let the Rotting of America Continue*."

Typical of the lead from behind mentality is "do not show your cards, because you may have to explain them." If we had an honest press, we would have heard the last of this but good Americans must remain vigilant as the press tires and tries again using anything but the truth to bring the President down.

Trump's $10 Billion in net worth did not come from watching others succeed. He breathes success. Only those who are both jealous of Trump and who choose to be blind see anything else than success. His whole life has been about real solutions while Obama and his former Secretary of State had become the # 1 problem in the US today. Trump takes no crap and he is solving that problem for sure every time he wakes up to begin a new day.

Trump does not know that he is executing the principles of R-R-R, as he just uses his natural entrepreneurial instincts. It is his own plan along with a dose of the R-R-R. His plan already has a lot of R-R-R in it, and thus it is good for America and we have already seen its impact and we are awaiting much more. .

Before he became President, Donald Trump had his plan ready to go. Let me skim some of the bog notions for you in the following section: Trump's well-conceived and well-articulated plan can be found all over the Internet as well as on the Trump Web Site https://www.donaldjtrump.com. This is the essence of the Tax plan:

TAX REFORM THAT WILL MAKE AMERICA GREAT AGAIN

The Goals Of Donald J. Trump's Tax Plan

Too few Americans are working, too many jobs have been shipped overseas, and too many middle class families cannot make ends meet. This tax plan directly meets these challenges with four simple goals:

Tax relief for middle class Americans: In order to achieve the American dream, let people keep more money in their pockets and increase after-tax wages.

Simplify the tax code to reduce the headaches Americans face in preparing their taxes and let everyone keep more of their money.

Grow the American economy by discouraging corporate inversions, adding a huge number of new jobs, and making America globally competitive again.

Doesn't add to our debt and deficit, which are already too large.

The Trump Tax Plan Is Revenue Neutral

The Trump tax cuts are fully paid for by: Reducing or eliminating most deductions and loopholes available to the very rich.

A one-time deemed repatriation of corporate cash held overseas at a significantly discounted 10% tax rate, followed by an end to the deferral of taxes on corporate income earned abroad.
Reducing or eliminating corporate loopholes that cater to special interests, as well as deductions made unnecessary or redundant by the new lower tax rate on corporations and business income. We will also phase in a reasonable cap on the deductibility of business interest expenses.

America needs a bold, simple and achievable plan based on conservative economic principles. This plan does that with needed tax relief for all Americans, especially the working poor and middle class, pro-growth tax reform for all sizes of businesses, and fiscally responsible steps to ensure this plan does not add to our enormous debt and deficit.

This plan simplifies the tax code by taking nearly 50% of current filers off the income tax rolls entirely and reducing the number of tax brackets from seven to four for everyone else. This plan also reduces or eliminates loopholes used by the very rich and special interests made unnecessary or redundant by the new lower tax rates on individuals and companies.

Inc. Tax Rate	Long Term Cap Gains Dividend Rate	Single Filers	Married Filers	Heads of Household
0%	0%	$0 to $25,000	$0 to $50,000	$0 to $37,500
10%	0%	$25,001 to $50,000	$50,001 to $100,000	$37,501 to $75,000
20%	15%	$50,001 to $150,000	$100,001 to $300,000	$75,001 to $225,000
25%	20%	$150,001 & up	$300,001 and up	$225,001 and up

The Trump Tax Plan: A Simpler Tax Code For All Americans

When the income tax was first introduced, just one percent of Americans had to pay it. It was never intended as a tax most Americans would pay. The Trump plan eliminates the income tax for over 73 million households. 42 million households that currently file complex forms to determine they don't owe any income taxes will now file a one-page form saving them time, stress, uncertainty and an average of $110 in preparation costs. Over 31 million households get the same simplification and keep on average nearly $1,000 of their hard-earned money.

For those Americans who will still pay the income tax, the tax rates will go from the current seven brackets to four simpler, fairer brackets that eliminate the marriage penalty and the AMT while providing the lowest tax rate since before World War II:

With this huge reduction in rates, many of the current exemptions and deductions will become unnecessary or redundant. Those within the 10% bracket will keep all or most of their current deductions. Those within the 20% bracket will keep more than half of their current deductions. Those within the 25% bracket will keep fewer deductions. Charitable giving and mortgage interest deductions will remain unchanged for all taxpayers.

Simplifying the tax code and cutting every American's taxes will boost consumer spending, encourage savings and investment, and maximize economic growth.

Business Tax Reform To Encourage Jobs And Spur Economic Growth

Too many companies – from great American brands to innovative startups – are leaving America, either directly or through corporate inversions. The Democrats want to outlaw inversions, but that will never work. Companies leaving is not the disease, it is the symptom. Politicians in Washington have let America fall from the best corporate tax rate in the industrialized world in the 1980's (thanks to Ronald Reagan) to the worst rate in the industrialized world. That is unacceptable. Under the Trump plan, America will compete with the world and win by cutting the corporate tax rate to 15%, taking our rate from one of the worst to one of the best.

This lower tax rate cannot be for big business alone; it needs to help the small businesses that are the true engine of our economy. Right now, freelancers, sole proprietors, unincorporated small businesses and pass-through entities are taxed at the high personal income tax rates. This treatment stifles small businesses. It also stifles tax reform because efforts to reduce loopholes and deductions available to the very rich and special interests end up hitting small businesses and job creators as well. The Trump plan addresses this challenge head on with a new business income tax rate within the personal income tax code that matches the 15% corporate tax rate to help these businesses, entrepreneurs and freelancers grow and prosper.

These lower rates will provide a tremendous stimulus for the economy – significant GDP growth, a huge number of new jobs and an increase in after-tax wages for workers.

Are there problems with the Trump Tax Plan?

The fact that Donald Trump's economic plan is designed well and that it will get America quickly out of its economic funk is verified by the Democratic Party, which early on took the time to write a hit piece on Trump's plan. Their "independent analysis," which has everything but credibility, predicted that Donald Trump's economic policies would plunge the United States into a deep recession. The lead author of the piece pursued a political agenda on behalf of the Democratic Party. Mark Zandi is so independent that he donated $2,700 last year to the Hillary Clinton Campaign.

Business school professor, Peter Navarro wrote a report that suggests the plan is solid in all respects. In fact, Navarro especially likes the immigration aspects. Deporting 11 million immigrants who have entered the United States illegally would not hurt the economy at all. Why? Because those illegal aliens would no longer draw public assistance and their jobs would almost immediately be taken by native-born Americans, particularly African-Americans. Navarro also noted that Trump's threat of high Tariffs (Mercantilism) on Chinese goods would force Chinese leaders to change their trading practices and eliminate their trade surplus with America. This would boost economic growth in the United States.

Navarro has contended that Trump's massive tax-cut plan will not cost the federal government a dollar in tax revenue. He notes that Trump is not about to pass a tax plan that loses money. "For the Trump tax plan, revenue neutrality is an important principle," Navarro said. "And that's where you start. That's the most important principle."

TRUMP TRADE PLAN: REFORMING THE U.S.-CHINA TRADE RELATIONSHIP TO MAKE AMERICA GREAT AGAIN

How We Got Here: Washington Politicians Let China Off The Hook

In January 2000, President Bill Clinton boldly promised China's inclusion in the World Trade Organization (WTO) "is a good deal for America." [It was not then and it is not now! He said that our products] "will gain better access to China's market, and every sector from agriculture, to telecommunications, to automobiles. But China gains no new market access to the United States." None of what President Clinton promised came true.

Since China joined the WTO, Americans have witnessed the closure of more than 50,000 US factories and the loss of tens of millions of jobs. Let me repeat. It was not a good deal for America then and it's a bad deal now. It is a typical example of how politicians in Washington have failed our country.

The most important component of our China policy is leadership and strength at the negotiating table. We have been too afraid to protect and advance American interests and to challenge China to live up to its obligations. We need smart negotiators who will serve the interests of American workers – not Wall Street insiders that want to move U.S. manufacturing and investment offshore.

The Goal of the Trump Plan: Fighting for American Businesses And Workers

America has always been a trading nation. Under the Trump administration trade will flourish. However, for free trade to bring prosperity to America, it must also be fair trade. Our goal is not protectionism but accountability. America fully opened its markets to China but China has not reciprocated. Its Great Wall of

Protectionism uses unlawful Tariff and non-tariff barriers to keep American companies out of China and to tilt the playing field in their favor.

If you give American workers a level playing field, they will win. At its heart, this plan is a negotiating strategy to bring fairness to our trade with China. The results will be huge for American businesses and workers. Jobs and factories will stop moving offshore and instead stay here at home. The economy will boom. The steps outlined in this plan will make that a reality.

When Donald J. Trump is president, China will be on notice that America is back in the global leadership business and that their days of currency manipulation and cheating are over. We will cut a better deal with China that helps American businesses and workers compete.

The Trump Plan Will Achieve The Following Goals:

✓ **Bring China to the bargaining table** by immediately declaring it a currency manipulator.

✓ **Protect American ingenuity and investment** by forcing China to uphold intellectual property laws and stop their unfair and unlawful practice of forcing U.S. companies to share proprietary technology with Chinese competitors as a condition of entry to China's market.

✓ **Reclaim millions of American jobs and reviving American manufacturing** by putting an end to China's illegal export subsidies and lax labor and environmental standards. No more sweatshops or pollution havens stealing jobs from American workers.

✓ **Strengthen our negotiating position** by lowering our corporate tax rate to keep American companies and jobs here at home, attacking our debt and deficit so China cannot use financial blackmail against us, and bolstering the U.S. military presence in the East and South China Seas to discourage Chinese adventurism.

Building Trump's R-R-R Plan

The first step in the process for me was in identifying each problem. The second part of the process was to devise can't miss solutions for each of the problems.

Ask yourself, "What were the biggest domestic problems facing the United States during the Obama Administration." Besides saying "Everything," it would help to discuss some specifics. Remember this was how it was in the pre-Trump days.

I bet your list (in no sequence) would not be too much different than mine:

1) Oppressive taxes stifle individual, national, and business creativity.
2) Legal and illegal immigrants take American jobs.
3) Regulations choke businesses; rob personal liberty & freedom.
4) Spending too much causes major deficits; creates huge national debt.
5) Big government health takeover adds taxes, spending; makes health worse.
6) America is now a de-industrialized, weaker nation.
7) Offshoring has stolen the best American jobs.
8) American corporations that offshore pay no Tariffs to home country (US).
9) Energy dependence unfriendly nations despite huge energy resources.
10) Redistribution of wealth and income = dependency on government.
11) Institutionalized government lying serves its selfish ends & cheats American people.
12) Massive government, massive payroll too expensive, intrusive, powerful.
13) Government and the people do not learn from our mistakes

This is too long a list of problems for any economy to withstand, and we could have probably added a lot more than a few more items to the list. But, if we can fix these big problems, few Americans would not agree that we can solve our economic woes and create an environment in which jobs pour into this nation from all across the world. Donald Trump is already doing this and his wise use of Tariffs is just one of his tools. We have to let him use the Tariff tool or eventually we will not be able to build anything in America.

With the 13 points above as my goal in the fall of 2011, as I prepared to launch my campaign for US Senate, I introduced R-R-R: a unique plan for economic recovery and job creation. In the spring of 2012, as discussed in early chapters, I wrote a book about it and during the active part of my campaign I gave speeches about the benefits of the R-R-R plan to America and to any candidate for any office, who might choose to adopt the plan.

You may recall that at the time, every conservative candidate was speaking a great game but nobody had anything solid to offer that had pizzazz and excitement built into their plans. Of course Herman Cain with his "9-9-9" plan was the exception. The fanfare was so great that many of us could have become convinced that 9-9-9 would be the next cure for insomnia or even halitosis. As much as a restructuring of our tax system is important for economic recovery, Herman Cain's 9-9-9 addresses just one of Donald Trump's economic recovery points.

In fact, it addresses just part of item one from the domestic problems list shown above. Yet, nobody denied that it was simply brilliant as a marketing concept. Out of nowhere, almost overnight, the former Burger King and Godfather Pizza executive was known to all Americans.

Even without 9-9-9, we know logically that taxes can be reduced simply by reducing the rates that are in effect in the out-of-touch 75,000 page tax code but clearly a proper code restructuring would help even more. Donald Trump's first cut at tax reform in 2018 accomplished most of the goals. Cain's winning strategy had more to do with a lot of pizzazz and his persona always came to the stage with a lot of moxie. Donald Trump is even better at marketing than Herman Cain, and that says something…and Trump is delivering.

Herman Cain showed us all that if we take a good solution and we add some panache and some zip; some spunk, splash, and zest to the mixture, soon the whole world will take notice and we will have ourselves a great solution. Everybody and their brothers and sisters all of a sudden knew about 9-9-9. Today everybody knows about the Trump Tax Cuts, especially after Nancy Pelosi suggested Americans give the government back their several thousand dollars in "tax crumbs." Who is she?

Besides the tax cut, Trump is moving us with Tariffs and negotiations out of free trade per se and into fair trade.

Ian Fletcher offers us a great perspective on the evils of free trade in his piece titled: "The Conservative Case Against Free Trade; Free Trade Doesn't Work."

"...But trade, and free trade are not the same thing. Remember that when somebody tries to tell you how wonderful free trade is: they're probably just giving arguments in favor of trade. Nobody on the protectionist side is suggesting we become North Korea, but there are very serious reasons why free trade is not sound economics, and the longer America clings to the free-trade delusion, the higher the price we will pay. Indeed, abandoning it is almost certainly a necessary, if not sufficient, condition for revitalizing our economy."

Donald Trump is taking America in the right direction. Levying Tariffs on those who have huge trade obstacles for American Trade is FAIR Trade. US Tariffs are a way to assure American industry will be available to make things and it is a way of making the whole world a fairer place to trade.

It is not that free trade is all bad. It is just not good for America and Americans. The R-R-R plan is about revitalizing the economy by reducing offshoring and creating more jobs on American soil. The precepts do include raising Tariffs so as not to reward American companies for moving factories and operations offshore; and to simply reindustrialize America for all of our collective benefit.

Free trade was working sometimes for large businesses that will do anything to make a profit. Listen to them squawk when Mr. Trump levies Tariffs on unfair trading partners. Big American moguls such as the Koch Brothers care not an iota about Americans but they do care a lot about the profits of the Koch machine. Remember that when you hear them disparage Tariffs. Selfish people do not want to lose their advantages over regular Americans.

The Koch's and those like them are not phonies. It would be wrong to call them phonies. They are honest people who want what is best for them and to hell with the rest of America. Don't let their honesty fool you and don't let their squawking about Trump sway you even a little. The Koch's have one interest – the Koch's. Donald Trump is for all Americans. He loves being our President despite how miserable the Never Trumpers, the Democrats, and the Press have made it for him. God gave us Donald trump. Please see the next chapter and I will expound on that idea.

If I were a politician advocating free trade, quite frankly I would be embarrassed. It is actually anti-American in what it does to bread-winners and families. I can understand Obama being an advocate, as he is for everything I am against. Obama for eight years was against everything that I am for so why change now as he leads the resistance.

As a final thought on free trade, when Barack Obama is really for something as he seemed to be with free trade, it disturbed me to see him hurting the economy with his bad deals. Free trade works only for the country that gains the markets and gains the jobs. It does not work for US. We took the worst of the worst and made them our lead negotiators.

Many who have read my columns know that I am a conservative Democrat, and so, I have gotten accustomed to saying things my party does not like. Quite frankly, I frequently say that "I don't like what my party says most of the time."

Unemployment is now hovering around 4% and the deficit has been over $Trillion each Obama year. Progressive Democrats did this to the rest of US! They must be replaced. Trump is getting things done despite the Democrats in Congress and the Never Trumpers. We have to get rid of them. No good changes will occur unless new faces with conservative, nationalist and pro-American ideas are brought in to Congress to help us all get the job done. But with Trump at the helm somehow we are able to move forward.

George Burns, one of America's all-time best comedians died in 1996 at 100 years of age. He was a shot way from playing the London Palladium, as he had predicted for many years before his 100th birthday. Like you and I, Burns was always concerned about the best people running the US government. Burns once quipped: "Too bad the only people who know how to run the country are busy driving cabs and cutting hair." R-R-R is not just for barber and cabbie chatter and economic recovery, it is for long-term success.

Mercantilism and Tariffs are necessary for the good of America. We need to move the US from pure capitalism to a modified capitalist / mercantilist economy. Elitists do not like mercantilism. They like free trade.

Maybe they are not so smart or maybe they do not care about regular people or America per se. Capitalism is a core ingredient of R-R-R mercantilism. R-R-R mercantilism is designed to help the home country. The home country in our case is the United States of America. The US needs the big bounce that R-R-R mercantilism with appropriate Tariffs can provide. Just announcing it as the plan will help continue the jump-start that Trump has already kicked-off.

The world currency

The United States still controls the world currency, though China has some markers on how long that bet will last. Conservatives and Nationalists and others who are paying attention know our nation under Obama was declining. Free trade & one-sided trade agreements are a major part of our problems.

Even my dog is smart enough to notice that if we replaced America's inept trade negotiators with a small pebble, a tsetse fly, a piece of guano, and an empty beer bottle, we would win more trade battles and the country would fare better overall. Other countries are eager to take our place as the world leader. Free trade gives them a license to do just that. Why argue for something that your foes will give you for nothing?

China wants its currency, the yuan, to replace the U.S. dollar as the world's global currency. That would give it more control over its economy. You can bet that is important to China and it makes Trump's tough stance on Tariffs v China as even more important.

As China's economic might grows, it's taking steps to make that happen. A slim majority of institutional investors see it as inevitable, but don't say when. Could we see a switch from a greenback- to a redback -dominated world? If so, how and when would that happen? What would be the consequences? We won't answer that in this book but remember the issue and remember why Trump is using Tariffs to outfox our trading partners and potential enemies such as China.

For every major political campaign, a great slogan is important for success. Remember these– *I like Ike.* -- *Are you better off now than you were four years ago?* -- *It's the economy, stupid* – *Compassionate conservativism,* -- And of course there are short ones, which live longer and perhaps never die—*9-9-9*, & now there is *R-R-R*.

Admittedly, sound ideas are more important than slogans. Adopting R-R-R to boost the American economy is a smart idea and Donald Trump is a very smart man.

England paid dearly in many ways for shifting from Mercantilism to free-trade. By 1944, the English pound officially lost its role as the reserve world currency. The US dollar took its place. The US still represents ¼ of the world market. And, we still control the currency? At least for now! For now, everybody wants to do business with US.

Free trade has been killing the US economy! The progressive President Wilson moved US away from mercantilism 100 years ago when he brought in the personal income tax. I bet there are not too many conservative fans of the personal income tax. In the days of mercantilism of old, a personal income tax was not needed, and it is not needed today if we were ready to refocus on consumption based methods such as the FAIR Tax or even 9-9-9.

It has taken 100 years for us to feel the full impact of free trade. And, it does not feel good. R-R-R mercantilism with real Tariffs as major tools puts the interests of the people of the US—the home country, ahead of the interests of strangers from other countries. It is specifically America first. The details of R-R-R mercantilism provide a huge carrot to encourage businesses to be good American "citizens." It also has a big stick to discourage American businesses from playing against the home country.

What real American is happy that we have given up over 20,000,000 manufacturing jobs to foreign countries? R-R-R mercantilism encourages companies to come home. If businesses choose not to come home to America, it will cost them, and it should cost them. Don't you agree?

In prior chapters, we touched on the problems for the future. Now, let's show some detail. Analysts predict that over the next decade or two, our not-so-loyal corporations will offshore another 40 million American jobs. The jobs we lose will be the best white-collar jobs that exist today—engineering jobs, accounting jobs, even radiologist's jobs and yes, doctors—even surgeons. You won't believe the projections. Tariffs can change all that.

Is it any wonder why our children, the hope of America, are graduating from great Universities only to come home with a huge debt and no job? Thank the free-trade crowd and the open borders crowd for that. We will get fair trade from Donald Trump and Mike Pence and we'll stop granting over six million visas a year, many of which are designed by Congress to take American jobs. The Trump, Pence, and Reform R-R-R is real enough to make America whole again.

Ironically, none of my doctors, who I trust implicitly with my health, trust the government to make the decisions about my health that they make today. Do you trust this government? More and more Americans are finding that even our best jobs can be offshored in an anything goes free trade society. It is happening all around us and when he was in office President Obama was the strongest advocate of free trade. Despite what Obama thinks, "Free trade doesn't work." Donald Trump knows that and with policy and Tariffs, he is already changing the game.

Has anybody asked how we can get back all the jobs that were exported in the last 30 years? The answer is that we must give businesses from across the world a major incentive to set up shop in America. The R-R-R plan does just that. If we want to re-industrialize America, we must also protect our markets and support our domestic industries. It is that simple. By the way, as noted earlier in this book, China practices Mercantilism. What do they know that we do not know? The Chinese love competing against Americans. Our trade negotiators before Trump always have chosen not to win. Trump is changing all that to benefit the United States.

We can't do it alone as citizens. We need a truly people-oriented representative Congress, President, and Vice president to help us get that job done. We got two out of the three, now when you vote for Congress, make sure you know where they stand on Tariffs and the rest of the Trump agenda. For years we had a self-absorbed President and corrupt representatives. Now we have a president who loves America and Americans and works every day to make America great and then greater. It would also be nice to have a trustworthy Congress working for the people and not just themselves. We can change everything that is bad just like we got ourselves a great president..

R-R-R mercantilism and Tariffs are tools that President Trump and a new people-oriented batch of new leaders in Congress can use to assure both survival and great success. Our job is to convince the both Houses of Congress R-R-R and Tariffs can not only save America; it can help America prosper for the long haul. With the ring it will bring when it is announced, it will be remembered and it will help guide conservatives to a well anticipated huge victory in November 2008. Let's all vote for the new R-R-R plan for America and Americans— First!

Chapter 6 Did God Give America Donald Trump?

I think God is a Trump supporter. I for one am very glad he (Trump) came along. Aren't you. I am going to stop right now and reprint an email I sent out the other day to remind my friends and relatives about my perception of Mr. Trump before the election.

Only those who choose not to see cannot see what is happening today with all the hate for this man. So, today I went back to the Wilkes-Barre Citizen's Voice Newspaper Archives and I found the letter to the editor that I sent in two months before the 2016 election. I am glad God heard my prayer.

Perhaps you will enjoy this as much as I enjoyed rereading it. Those who stand still when they have the chance to act in God's favor often regret their inaction. I am tickled and proud of myself that despite seemingly popular sentiments, I was inspired to write this brief piece and send it in. If I could only open some hearts along the way, perhaps we could diffuse some of the hate. After all, we are all Americans and thus we should all be for the best for America.

Here is what I sent:

LETTER TO THE EDITOR / PUBLISHED: SEPTEMBER 11, 2016 WB CITIZENS Voice

There are many billionaires who want things their way on taxes and they figure they will benefit if their lobbyists get to the right politician. Donald Trump is actually running for office as a billionaire. He does not need a job. Yet, he is investing a lot of time in America. He does not need it. But, if he is successful, his kids will grow up in America and he wants it to be the finest country of any possible country ever. Bravo, Donald Trump.

Mr. Trump wants it to be like the America as founded by honest founders. Donald Trump is intrinsically honest. He may round up on some issues in his favor but he is not corrupt. He wants his kids to love him and respect him just like you want your kids to think of you.

We are only on Earth for a short time. Why should we not do our best? I love that Donald Trump, a billionaire who needs me like a hole in the head, thinks I matter. He thinks you matter. He thinks America matters. He thinks God matters. He is right on all points. Unlike you and me, he has the means and the opportunity to really show God and his family what a good man he really is.

We have been waiting for you, Mr. Trump, since Ronald Reagan left us. God gave us Donald Trump. I am convinced that it is up to us to make him our president. We did not know how bad the Bushes were until they went into their recent crying tantrum because they lost. We just know that they were not too good when they had the power. Donald Trump is bombastic, arrogant when he knows he is right, and he is often inartful in his speech when he is upset. However, he, like my father, is a very good man. I welcome the opportunity to cast my vote for him. I thank God for the opportunity.

Brian W. Kelly

Wilkes-Barre

Chapter 7 Reduce the Corporate Income Tax via Tariffs

Reduce Corporate Taxes to 8 Per Cent or Lower

In the final version of the Tax Cuts and Jobs Act of 2017, that Trump was signed into law December 22 , 2017, year, Congress voted to lower the corporate income tax from 35% to 21% with the corporate rate taking effect immediately in 2018. This is one of the mini engines among many that have helped the economy take off to a 4.1% GDP in the 2nd quarter. In my opinion, this is not enough. The Corporate Income Tax is not a big money raiser for the country.

Many Democrats do not seem willing to admit that John F. Kennedy was a tax cutter. Not one Democrat in the house or Senate voted to reduce the people's taxes. President Kennedy cut the personal and corporate tax rates as one of his first actions as president. Why? Because Kennedy was not a doofus as his family had made their money in business and he did not depend on a corrupt press to prop up his status.

Kennedy was pro-American and so when taxes needed to be cut, he was ready to do so for the American cause. Like Trump, and his children, JFK was the product of successful parents. In 1962, always a favorite of Democrats and also many Republicans, President JFK favored tax reduction in a big way. His cuts are well remembered. Kennedy had a great way with words. Those of us old enough and those who are historians may remember these Kennedy words:

"In short, it is a paradoxical truth that … the soundest way to raise the revenues in the long run is to cut the rates now… And the reason is that only full employment can balance the budget, and tax reduction can pave the way to that employment. The purpose of cutting taxes now is not to incur a budget

deficit, but to achieve the more prosperous, expanding economy which can bring a budget surplus."

JFK was wise beyond his years. Today, the JFK philosophy would be identified as *conservative.* The fact is that when Trump was elected, our economy had gotten sick again just like in Kennedy's time. So we needed to put more pay in employee's pockets with a permanent tax fix. What Congress did was create temporary tax cuts that is why Trump is going back for round 2 and again Democrats are standing in his way.

Recently, a coalition of the unlikely--organizations including liberal groups and labor unions have been urging lawmakers to reject a potential second round of tax cuts, as the there is a notion that they may become law before the election. Why labor unions do not want their membership to pay less taxes is a conundrum for me. The fake news media is all over this posting stories that are mostly lies hoping to convince Americans to vote to give back the money they have saved. They say it benefits the rich only but this is not true as all Americans have gained as much as multiple thousands of dollars in tax relied.

Here is a typical fake new blast full of lies:

"America cannot afford the Trump-GOP tax cuts benefitting the rich and corporations, and we sure cannot afford a Round 2 that puts the interests of the wealthy over everyone else while maintaining a lower tax rate on income earned from wealth compared to wages and salaries," the groups noted above wrote this week in a letter to Congress members.

The President signed a tax-cut bill in December that cut rates for individuals and businesses. The same officials want to tackle another package of tax cuts before the midterm elections.

House Republicans say they are aiming to vote on a second round of tax cuts this fall—among other things to make the cuts permanent. Skeptics say that a second tax bill is unlikely to pass the Senate, where it would need 60 votes. Robert Casey of PA who I am running against for the US Senate in November will vote no on the cuts. If I were in office, I would vote YES.

As noted the Republican top priority for a second round of tax cuts is to make the cuts for individuals in last year's bill permanent. The individual cuts expire after eight years in order to comply with rules that allowed Republicans to avoid a Democratic filibuster.

Supporters of phase two of the tax cuts argue that making the individual tax cuts permanent would help middle-class families. The bill lowers tax rates across the board and increases the standard deduction and child tax credit. Unless they want to give a lot more to the government, Americans should be for the tax cuts.

Liberal groups and unions feel differently because they are afraid Trump will take credit for the cuts and nothing good for Trump, even if it helps the people, is good for the Democrats. Groups that signed the letter include Americans for Tax Fairness, Tax March and the AFL-CIO.

What Americans do not want or need is to put more pay in freeloader's pockets for purposes, which Governor Christie suggests include being a couch potato, perhaps smothered in French Fries and gravy. When you pay people for not working, you get a lot more looking for the same pay for the same work. Why unions are telling their members to vote to let others stay on the couch is not in the American spirit. Nobody wants to hire a gravy smothered French-fried couch potato for productive work.

Donald Trump wanted to cut the personal income tax max to 25% and the corporate tax to 15%. I am OK with the personal rate cut but the corporate cut at 21% as passed needs to be greater. The fact is with all the loopholes for corporations, the corporate tax rate can be brought to 5% with no loopholes – every corporation pays the same rate, and the revenue would be the same or perhaps even more. Corporations will flock home from overseas with a 5% rate.

Ron Paul says that "One thing is clear: The Founding Fathers never intended a nation where citizens would pay nearly half of everything they earn to the government." With 46% of Americans paying no tax at all, how is that a good deal for this country? In the R-R-R plan everybody pays at least 1%. Everybody pays the personal income tax and nobody pays less than 1% and nobody gets a refund greater than their withheld tax.

The US Tax Code is a taxpayers' joke and a lobbyists dream. With over 75,000 pages of exemptions and exceptions, written by lobbyists with a lot to gain, it has been a public outrage and nightmare. All corporate welfare and subsidies must be eliminated. There is room for a round 2 and a round 3 and even further rounds to reduce the code and to reduce the tax burden.

Tariffs can offset any extra cash that winds up in your pocket. Better than having a ton of tax money coming in to the treasury, lawmakers need to figure out how to reduce spending and then the people can have their tax cut and no Democrat will be out there saying that the tax code cannot afford the tax cut. Hooey!

The best way to do it is to restructure the entire tax code with permanent changes. This is going to happen because it is what the President desires as do most of the regular people in America.

Are you not pleased that Donald Trump and Mike Pence are fighting to make all men equal again. In all the great work done so far in Trump's turn none can be so great as minorities such as African Americans and Hispanics enjoying the lowest unemployment rate in modern times That is what good trade and tax policies bring to America.

Nobody should pay for anybody else unless they are hurting or on disability. Cases of beer for the front porch while the rest of the city is working is not something that should be funded. The Constitution written by the founders has nothing in it about giving your earnings to somebody else.

Do corporate income taxes really matter?

They matter a lot less than in the 1950's; that is for sure. In the 1950's, the Federal Corporate Income Tax provided 30% of the country's revenue. Now, with more powerful corporations than ever, and lobbyists demanding more and more favors from politicians, there are so many deductions and subsidies for corporations that the effective corporate tax now provides just 6.5% of federal revenue. If it provides so little revenue, why make those corporations without the big accountants and lawyers pay the full 35% in their tax returns? In 2018 of course, the rate is now 21% but that is still too high and the deductions are still there for big corporations with fat-cat lawyers and accountants.

Corporations, the same corporations that demanded citizenship long ago, need to now earn that citizenship by becoming more American. Reducing the corporate tax rate will attract foreign investment and it will incent American corporations to produce in America. That is the carrot and the stick of course is a 35% Tariff on goods manufactured overseas and sold in America. You can see the value of Tariffs in getting corporations to do the right thing.

Of course, the overarching objective of reducing the corporate tax rate is to have more jobs in America. Any revenue lost from such a cut will come back by the taxation of the ample dividends that will be paid when the corporate cash is actually distributed to needy stockholders. Additionally products imported to the US by US forms will pay through the nose and what they pay will go into the US Treasury.

The corporate tax impact on the Federal Government's success in raising revenue is minimal. We make too big a deal out of it. We are talking about just 6.5% of revenue. Reducing the tax rate to an awesomely small amount— 8% or less—without permitting special deductions or subsidies, will continue to provide substantial revenue to the treasury—perhaps even more than we get today. Revenue from corporations would go up by restructuring the code and reducing the rate, and don't forget that dividends would be taxed at the normal tax rate.

Donald Trump is on the right track as he wants the corporate tax to go to 15% from about 21% (just reduced from 35% in 2018). Though I think 8% is somewhat low, I would lower the corporate tax even further to 5% so that taxation is never a reason for corporations to take jobs overseas. Even huge corporations would pay the full 5% and the total revenue would be more than today, and all companies would be treated fairly –large and small.

Overall, a restructuring of the corporate tax rate as part of an overall Round 3 tax restructuring is the best notion. Donald Trump is for this restructuring. Taxes should be broad-based and the rates should be relatively low. In terms of the R-R-R plan, our objective is not just to reduce the rates so US corporations can be more profitable, it is to attract US corporations to once again operate their businesses in America without having to penalize them.

Our tax system is not perceived to be fair because it has not been fair. As of December 2017, it is fairer but it is still not fair and it does not give US industry a massive competitive advantage. You may recall that just a few years ago, GE made billions of dollars and paid no corporate income tax. Additionally GE got a $3 billion rebate. We surely do not need a corporate tax system that costs the country money. Cut out rebates which are nothing more than corporate welfare.

The advocacy group Citizens for Tax Justice recently released a report detailing 15 Fortune 500 companies that don't pay any taxes. Nice deal if you can get it! Guess who is on the list. It is not just Ge but yes GE is on the list.

The list includes CBS, General Electric, Interpublic Group, JetBlue Airways, Mattel, Owens Corning, PG&E, Pepco Holdings, Priceline.com, Prudential Financial, Qualcomm, Ryder System, Time Warner, Weyerhaeuser and Xerox. Why bother. Get rid of all corporate loopholes and maybe the dishonest lobbyists will disappear from Washington at the same time. That would reduce the need for deodorant in the social gathering spots in DC.

As a whole, the 15 companies paid no federal income tax on $23 billion in profits in 2014, and they paid almost no federal income tax on $107 billion in profits during the past five years. All but two received federal tax rebates in 2014, and almost all paid exceedingly low rates over five years. So, reduce the tax rate to 5%. This will bring corporations home to America.

The most important factor is to create a tax system so that companies from all over the world, including American businesses that have offshored operations, will want to do business again by manufacturing and creating jobs in the new Trump America.

The new America will be a business bonanza in which corporate / business taxes are low, yet government revenue is the same and more than likely greater. If we do our best with the R-R-R plan, and companies like Apple, a company that grossed about $250 Billion last year choose not to come back–fine! It is time that America began to worry about American citizens before corporations. We'll get Apple's share via Mercantilism. Now we all know how to spell the word *Tariff.*

Reduce the domestic corporate tax rate to 5%

I'd like corporate tax to be zero... but I fear that smart manipulators would come up with ways that this rate would not benefit America. One percent would be better than zero because I want there to be a mechanism to collect taxes if we guess wrong and things do not go as expected and we need an easy source of revenue.

If American Corporations won't employ Americans, foreign corporations in America will!

Of course, a big carrot for business is to reduce the corporate tax rate to 8% or5% or less for both domestic corporations and foreign corporations. Because this plan is about putting Americans back to work in good jobs, foreign companies that build plants and offices in America and who hire Americans will also get the reduced tax rate and a big thank you from the new Trump Federal Government that operates to help, not hurt Americans.

Like me, many Americans are unhappy that so many "faux American" corporations walked away from the United States and left so many unemployed in their wake. My recommendation is that nothing special be done for any American company that decides to come back because of R-R-R or for any other reason.

I would also say no special punishment should be meted. However, I would like to see corporations on their own choosing to set up funds for good American causes. For example, it would be nice if corporations used some of their tax savings to help students pay for their student loans, or to help state unemployment funds stay afloat, or to provide some free goods to charity. For these kind works, American corporations should receive thank you's and major kudos from a government that operates for the people as well as from the people ourselves.

Many know that corporations originally gained their American personhood in the famous 1886 Supreme Court case called *Santa Clara County v. Southern Pacific*. The founders never wanted to give corporations an inch. In fact, they were illegal after the Revolution for many years. Give them an inch and they will take a mile. Can you imagine that there were debates on personhood by the founders about corporations?

About 100 years after the Constitution, the slippery slope saw corporations emerged in America from minimal entities to having more power than even the monopolistic British East India Company, the bane of the colonists. The founders would have thrown over the Tea a number of additional times, rather than ever give in to corporate personhood.

Look what has happened. Other than corporate officers or stockholders; what person in America, has really gained from the existence of corporations. Corporations over the last thirty years have stolen away a lot of what makes America—America, simply by pure greed. They used their large purses to buy politicians. They have taken our jobs and much of our strength as a country and they have diminished America's standing in the world.

I know Donald Trump runs powerful corporations but he does not need as much as a CEO or a CFO who does not own the company. Trump knows how to make sure the people get no more but more importantly, no less than their due.

Since becoming persons, US Corporations have simply been bad American citizens to say the least. As real flesh bearing persons, *We the People* are challenged to take control of our government, which was founded to be *Of the People* and *By the People*. Bringing Donald Trump in as our President was a wonderful beginning.

Corporations are so much more powerful as entities than individuals, and in America, other than corporations, no group is endowed with any real power. We are a country of individuals, and only if we have an honest government do things go well for Americans. Enough said! Mr. Trump, has delivered so far on an honest government. For that he gets the kudos.

Because the Constitution gives us strength, with the right leadership, we can implement the R-R-R plan. This takes back power from corporations and it pays them back somewhat with a substantially lower corporate tax rate. I sincerely hope that corporations do choose to become much better citizens. And for that, I will be the first to sing their praises. If not, then we must elect politicians, even those who do not think they are political such as Donald Trump, who understand the purpose of the stick rather than the carrot.

The 8% or 5% or less domestic corporate tax rate is a phenomenal tax reduction which will especially help the good corporations that have been using American employees to produce goods and / or provide services here in America. The US foreign tax on American corporations should also be reduced but to no less than 20%. Those corporations operating in America should pay less taxes…period! As noted, I think 5% is a good number.

The foreign rate would be reduced from 35% to 21% to simplify the tax code and eliminate the foreign tax credits that have been overly abused over the years. The higher rate (20% v 5%) on overseas profits is meant to incent companies to come back and make products at home. Corporations that leave the US for 50 years should have Tariffs on all their imports. Do you see how Tariffs are good for America.

A 5 to 8 percent or less domestic corporate tax rate v 21 or 35% may induce some offshore-centric companies to come back home. But, realistically, it may not be enough to have all corporations fall in line, and so for those who want to continue offshore, we offer the stick of mercantilism instead of the carrot.

Another big goodie on the carrot side for firms or portions of firms operating in the United States will be the opportunity for direct expensing of all costs. No depreciation schedules should be necessary. If you buy something, take the full credit that year. For firms manufacturing overseas, however, the schedules should continue to be used. Why make it easy for companies that make it harder for US citizens? This is another way to encourage US plant expansion in the US and we hope this too will be a carrot to help bring businesses back.

Of course, no corporation should receive subsidies for anything. No corporation should receive anything any other company cannot get. All corporations will therefore play by the same rules. Those that operate their businesses in the US will receive major benefits, available to all companies, and those operating overseas will not receive as many benefits if any.

Another important R-R-R incentive, *Reduce Regulations* will eliminate business stifling rules and this will assure that no company ever gets punished by the government for setting up shop in America. This is another notion that will surely help bring jobs back. President Trump has already enjoyed great success in this area and this has helped in the current economic boom.

If we don't get businesses to return to operating in America by using the carrot, the new America will get them back to America on the stick and it won't be because of the song, "Why—cause we love you!." It will become more expensive for American firms that use employees offshore – whether the industry is service or manufacturing to sell their wares in the USA. The tool we will use is the Tariff. Tariffs are good for America.

Yes, the sticks will be big and they must be big for the incentive to come back to be overwhelming. The objective of the goodies, such as tax cuts is not to be nice to corporations. It is to bring America back to being a country that can support a prosperous middle class.

In the R-R-R plan, the notion called *Reindustrializing America* is intended to bring back industries and plenty of plant jobs, engineering and IT jobs, as well as other good jobs. They will come back home because the carrots and sticks (tariffs) in R-R-R style Mercantilism will assure companies that it is their best option.

R-R-R Mercantilism with our recently adopted new friend *the Tariff,* will provide the incentive for formerly all-American corporations that have strayed to other countries for profits, to change their ways and think America-first. Historian Newt Gingrich would agree that this is the first time in world history that Tariff protectionism needs to be invoked to help the people, rather than the domestic industries.

The secret objective of R-R-R Mercantilism is thus to protect Americans from American corporations and other large unincorporated businesses that have taken jobs offshore. The mantra of R-R-R Mercantilism is that you are not an American corporation if you have moved your American jobs overseas.

Give foreign corporations explicit permission to beat unfaithful American corporations

Since American companies may not be motivated to return jobs to our country,   R-R-R Mercantilism encourages foreign companies to build plants and offices right here in America, where they can then hire American employees. It is that simple. Perhaps we even take away patent protection in the US for companies that stubbornly make their wares offshore. Foreign companies who know the iPhone patents could then make their clones in the US and pay less taxes than American companies abroad. Why not. Without America, how successful would Apple be?

For those "faux American" companies that choose to make their products offshore, Americans will benefit from a higher foreign corporate tax rate and from a Tariff on imported products. So, corporations can go right ahead and do as much as they find profitable for all goods imported to the US from the country of manufacture will find the stick. The Tariff stick will be huge and it will not lead to greater profits. But, it will help the US treasury

What sticks are you talking about?

One stick is that the tax rate on dollars earned by US corporations overseas, which includes any products shipped to the US or anywhere else, does not get the 5 to 8% or lower domestic American corporate tax rate. Instead it is a 20% straight tax over and above whatever tax is due to the foreign country. No discounts.

The foreign and domestic tax rates had been 35% for years (now 21%) but corporations have been able to deduct the foreign taxes paid to the host country in calculating their bill. In this plan, since the rate is lower to accommodate the foreign tax, there would be no deduction for the foreign tax.

In the unlikely event that American corporations choose to revolt and decide to unregister their corporate charter in the US, perhaps a third tier of income tax and an even higher Tariff would be imposed on faux American corporations that continue to make their products overseas but are no longer registered in the US. Perhaps their penalty box lasts for fifty years before it can be appealed. Such companies can choose to simply grin and bear it for their tax situation will not improve until they return to the US as a major industrial form.

The government of this United Sates under the R-R-R plan will be charged with publishing the list of "faux American" corporations that have abandoned their American Corporate Charter for the sake of higher profits. Perhaps with a loyal American population, no additional fees would need to be extracted as Americans may be upset enough to simply choose to use the products of loyal American corporations, or foreign firms that build in America rather than those that care little about America.

The R-R-R plan handles corporations that choose to behave in an un-American fashion. It demands that the US must pull the economic hammer down on such businesses to help the American people.

Therefore, any "faux American" business that chooses to revolt against Americans, may find things getting worse profit-wise for their companies if they choose to continue to sell in America. Remember the R-R-R mantra implicitly is America for Americans. It is America first and all other countries second.

Government, corporations and unions come far later in the pecking order, well after individual Americans. I would recommend that the names of any newly unregistered corporation be placed on a large placard outside the Department of Commerce Building in

Washington DC for all Americans to see. It is time to bring back public shame.

A similar notion can be developed for services, such as offshored call center work, and any other service that is moved from our shores to other shores. The objective of R-R-R Mercantilism is to create prosperity in America by helping the American people be prosperous by having better work opportunities. If corporations, American or otherwise choose to play ball with US, they should be very successful because of R-R-R Mercantilism while American employees regain their prominence in the world.

Tariffs R good for America

One more stick, upon which we have lightly touched, is Tariffs. Tariffs have traditionally been the heart of any mercantilist system from time immemorial. All of the R-R-R moves, from restructuring the tax code, reducing offshoring, reducing regulations, and raising Tariffs are designed to help reindustrialize America using the basic principles of mercantilism. This means we adopt principles that bring back higher paying jobs for Americans – especially our forgotten college graduates.

To do this right, just like as the founders prescribed, Tariffs will again be in play. I would expect there should be at least a 20% Tariff (maybe higher) on American goods imported into the US from American corporations and perhaps all imports from foreign corporations. With a little design, this process can be made to fit outsourced services as well. While corporations plan to outsource US all to other countries, under R-R-R mercantilism, it will not be cost free.

Since American citizens control the government, and not vice versa, it is up to the citizens via our representatives to assure that there are big-time costs for any company that executes a perdition strategy on America. When Americans set the tax rates and Tariffs differently for such companies, these companies will find out first hand that such a strategy is not really so good for the sponsoring corporation.

This will give our loyal domestic producers protection from foreign businesses. In one set of calculations that I performed, after a phased in approach, the R-R-R package would add as much as $500 billion to the treasury per year, while more importantly, it will stage the US for reindustrialization and much better jobs for all of our citizens.

America is a huge market for all corporations

We must remember that the American market represents ¼ of the world's market. Once a company is here, ¼ of the world's buyers are at its disposal. Companies can do quite well concentrating on America first and treating Americans fairly. No company that is in its right mind; would not want to participate in the American marketplace.

In the last thirty years and more obviously, in the last ten years, American companies have forgotten their loyal American employees and they have chosen higher profit opportunities elsewhere. The new tax code and the Tariffs, and other elements of R-R-R as discussed in this book, will bring a lot of industry back to the US along with lots of the best American jobs that many believed never would return. The survival instincts of formerly disloyal American corporations will compel them to come back and begin to behave better.

In the unlikely event that American based corporations dig in and choose not to come back at an acceptable level, they will miss out on an opportunity to participate in the best business climate in the world. Their places at the table will no longer be reserved for them. Their former reserved and protected spots will be filled by foreign enterprises who manufacture on our shore, not offshore. That will make up the shortfall and give Americans the job opportunities they have been denied by "faux American" corporations.

Foreign corporations have proven they can be a blessing as we have seen in recent years with the auto industry. A good look at these foreign companies over these years and even prudent conservatives would conclude they have done more for Americans than the "faux corporations" that have left, lock, stock, and barrel, with misery in their wake.

In my humble opinion, a foreign based company that sets up shop in America and hires Americans at a decent wage is a more American-like business than a so-called American Corporation that hires foreigners in foreign countries to make products and then it ships them back here duty free. R-R-R Mercantilism says the duty free days for such faux American corporations are gone. If you want to be treated as an American, be good to America. Tariffs are a great friend to America.

There are a number of other notions that go along with reducing taxes in a really fair way. The R-R-R plan, the formula for making America greater, accommodates all and delivers insights powerful enough to help us know that all facets need to be revamped to be fair.

This includes the personal income tax structure; the possibility of a Fair Tax; repercussions from a zero to humungous capital gains tax, and of course the other precepts of an honest and fair corporate tax, which includes solving the foreign income and tax deferral problem. All of these income / taxation notions and dilemmas are examined in this book. I bet you can't wait to digest all of what you have learned in this book. I could not wait to write it. That's why it is here now.

Remember Tariffs with a capital T, are your friend.

Chapter 8 Donald Trump Would Love Brian Kelly's US Senate Platform

Note from your author and Senate Candidate Brian W. Kelly

Brian Kelly when Chief Technology Officer College Misericordia circa 1994

No, I don't look like this anymore, but I did look like this when as the chief technology officer at College Misericordia in the 1990's, I began to pay a lot more attention to what goes on in our government. The College paid for this picture.

By now, I admit that I am not too happy with what I discovered about government and politics in our country. That, and because like you, I could not afford a full-bore Senatorial campaign, is why I am running as a write-in candidate for the US Senate.

Ask yourself this question: Would you hire any Congressman in America today to run your business—even to babysit your kids? Me neither! Yet, we hire them through the electoral process to run the most complex country that ever was—the United States of America. It is clear that at some point we must begin to make better choices. Why not start in 2018?

I think the best way to begin this chapter is to give you the announcement speech for the US Senate that I will give the first time I am given a forum in a cost-free venue. There is a lot in this speech but then again, there are many issues today in America. The issues addressed include solutions for resident illegal foreign nationals, Fair COLAs for Seniors, and a major economic stimulus by solving the student loan crisis.

As I review the contents of this speech below, I wish that I could make the speech shorter and at the same time more comprehensive, so you fully know what the platform is all about and why it is worthy of your consideration. I have done my best, but I do admit that this is not one of my shortest speeches. Thank you.

Originally, I wrote this speech for Congressman Lou Barletta of Pennsylvania, hoping he would adopt the platform elements in this speech as his own. I believe the Congressman likes these ideas but as he is running for Senator as a Republican, it would be difficult to convincing officials in the Republican Party of their worth. It would be tough to push a platform that may have a negative effect on the budget cuts Republicans are seeking. And, so, I decided to go it alone, and instead of expecting the man who I believe may still become Senator Barletta present these ideas for America, I will do the job myself under my own write-in candidacy for Democrat voters.

Yet, please, if you must vote Democrat in this election, remember that unlike Bob Casey Jr., I am not a Chuck Schumer or Nancy Pelosi Democrat nor am I a Maxine Watters Democrat nor do I stand for any principle such as the abolishment of ICE that harms the country I love. I would be pleased to accept your vote of confidence for my candidacy. Just write me in.

B-R-I-A-N   K-E-L-L-Y

Don't type the dashes.

Campaign Update August 3, 2018

This is the day after the Donald Trump Rally in Wilkes-Barre, my home town, on behalf of Republican Lou Barletta for the US Senate. As a result of that 1 hour and sixteen-minute rally, Donald Trump's phenomenal speech, his endorsement of Lou Barletta, and an equally great and inspiring speech by Senate Candidate Lou Barletta, I have decided to endorse Congressman Lou Barletta for the US Senate. I am as much **opposed** to Senator Robert 'Sleepin Bob' Casey as I am **in favor** of a great American, Lou Barletta, a man who shares most of my values.

For those Democrats who historically will not vote for a Republican under any circumstances, or those Democrats desiring the package of unique pro-American legislation that I have developed in the past, I encourage you to make a better choice for the US Senate than Bob Casey. Pennsylvania needs a great US Senator. Casey has not been that man and his concern for the people is getting worse, not better. Lou Barletta is the best choice. However, if you must vote Democrat, remember that Bob Casey is not for the people of Pennsylvania. Rather than vote for Casey, you may feel free to write my name in for United States Senator B-R-I-A-N   K-E-L-L-Y. I am a registered Democrat. Thank you.

At the PA Wilkes-Barre Rally, President Trump and Congressman Barletta netted out the same negative case against Bob Casey, Jr as a legislator. Trump began by saying the younger Casey was boring, a nobody in Washington who does what Democratic leaders tell him. I don't think I ever met him, Trump said. Bob Casey is for open borders, Trump asserted, again raising the specter of violent immigrants from Central America overrunning the country.

Barletta and Trump noted that Casey is a pro-abortion, anti-second amendment socialist by his record and he expects Casey to be calling for the abolition of the Immigration and Customs Enforcement (ICE) agency, a favorite cause on the left. He more or less said that Chuck Schumer says "Jump," and Bob Casey says: "How high?" Then, every, time, he goes ahead and jumps. Though Casey says he is not anti-ICE, he also says he is anti-abortion and then votes pro-abortion in almost all cases, such as his opposition to Judges Gorsich and Cavanaugh. For twelve years, Bob Casey Jr. has been the epitome of a do-nothing politician, choosing not to do the peoples business. It is time for Casey to make a graceful exit.

Like me, Lou Barletta is for the entire Trump agenda, especially the Wall, and that will be good for America. The only thing that we disagree on is a detailed solution that I put together in several books this year that squarely address resident illegal foreign nationals, Fair COLAs for Seniors, and a major economic stimulus by solving the student loan crisis.

End of Aug 3, 2018 Campaign Update

This speech, which I wrote for the announcement of my write-in candidacy for the office of US Senator from Pennsylvania offers great solutions for Obamacare, Immigration, Seniors and Social Security, and Millennials and Student Loans.

With this speech, I am able to show off a platform that can make seniors and millennials whole, fix the problem with illegal foreign nationals in the shadows, remove the need for sanctuary cities, and the problems with DACA, and help Americans afford health care insurance again. Added to the other Trump items such as Tariffs as an economic tool, this platform is unbeatable when the message gets out in the public arena.

The people will love this platform because it solves a ton of problems and puts bucks in many folk's pockets. Many US citizens from young to old have forgotten how nice a dollar looks.

God bless all of you who have purchased and read this book. Now you can enjoy the speech announcing Brian Kelly's candidacy for the US Senate against two-term Democratic incumbent Robert P. Casey Jr.   It is so right on for today that I enjoy it every time I read or edit it.

As you will see in the beginning of the speech, I designed it for an audience full of people. I have already had a positive reaction to my running for the US Senate as a Democrat alternative to Bob Casey from people in my inner circle.

Here is the speech preamble followed by unique platform points:

Fellow Citizens,

Language is inadequate to express my gratitude for the privilege of submitting before you my candidacy to represent the fine people of Pennsylvania as your US Senator.

I would also like to thank you for the fine welcome, which you all have extended to me on this occasion. As I look out in my mind's eye, I see a vast sea of human faces who share a common interest, as do I, about the greatest questions of our times. Beyond occasionally agitating the mind, they now dominate the concerns of all Pennsylvanians and U.S. citizens, underlying the foundations of our free institutions. Let us all make sure that freedom never becomes just another word for nothing left to lose.

The reaction of my U.S. Senate candidacy by the people of Pennsylvania has been quite heartening. We have a president whose interest quite simply is to "Make America Great Again." By contrast, the embedded establishment and liberal leftovers in the SWAMP, have no interest in performing what is good for our country. They are doing their best to undermine our president, without any repercussions, aided and abetted by a corrupt media, instead of building bridges to work for the good of all Americans.

It is no longer acceptable for a Democrat or a Republican to be a Never-Trumper. Donald Trump is our president and his platform is my platform and when elected, I hope the extras in my platform that I introduce in this speech, become part of the Trump platform.

We all know that "Never-Trumpers" will never hold office again. Democrats such as Bob Casey Jr., my opponent, simply adore the establishment's impediments to the president's agenda with a media whose interests are as adverse to the American people as the British press was during Colonial Times.

The Democrats and the Republican Never-Trumpers in the Senate, House, and the federal bureaucracy and the degenerate mainstream press have done everything they can to thwart the will of 62,979,636 people who voted to clean out the SWAMP with a fresh new presidential administration.

The legendarily venal Hillary Clinton lost the election after the public saw through her charade; yet she continues to parade around the world blaming everything from her own adoring fans at The New York Times, to white women like her, to the DNC, and probably even the cows in Wisconsin, a state she famously lost after taking it so for granted, she never visited.

She even blames the FBI and it never occurs to anyone that the best way to avoid an untimely FBI intervention in a political campaign is to *not run for President while under federal criminal investigation*. And all the while, Senator Casey stood by submissively, applauding and enabling this farce of a candidacy. It is time for the country to move on. She lost, now get over it. We've had twelve years of Casey and that's about as much as any man or woman in America can stand.

I am running for the US Senate to reclaim this seat which rightfully belongs to its people, not the extrinsic interests controlling our politicians who would tear the Constitution in half without hesitation if it would please their donors and cheerleaders in the mainstream media. Despite the shameless lack of virtue that defines the top echelons of our government, our country itself is replete with honest citizens who would be humbled to work on behalf of their fellow countrymen and women. That is why I am running for the US Senate against one of the biggest icons of mainstream mediocrity and corruption, Mr. Bob Casey Jr.

Casey Jr. caters only to the whining anti-Trump crowd who wants to turn every trivial post on Facebook into a new Cuban Missile Crisis. Despite the voters in even his home state rejecting the rank duplicity of former Secretary Clinton and her bleak vision of hopelessness and sovereign state decline, Senator Casey never lifted a finger to help the people who support our president, despite the fact that we outnumber the opposition right here in Pennsylvania. But to him-- that's Bob Casey, folks; we do not even exist.

The Bob Casey Jr. that we all see is a do-nothing Senator who would prefer to turn the US into a globalist abyss rather than support its sovereignty or its people's dignity. Meanwhile, our great president is trying to find everybody a high-paying job by making it easier to conduct business in our country. I intend to help President Trump protect us from such parasitic interests.

If there is one principle most cherished in all free governments, it is that which asserts the exclusive right of a free people to form and adopt their own fundamental laws, to manage and regulate their own internal affairs and domestic institutions. That is under constant attack by Mr. Casey and his legions of Clinton dead-enders.

Electing representatives of the people is not a triviality, but rather the expression of the most fundamental right of self-government. Without it, of course, this great United States would be like any other country in the world. It would not be the exceptional republic, which we the people have enjoyed since our own Declaration of Independence.

To say that I am honored to be here today presenting my candidacy for the US Senate, would be the understatement of the ages. Thank you for your reception and hospitality. I assure you that if elected, I will provide Pennsylvania and the United States of America the best representation in the US Senate of which I am capable. You can be sure of that.

We have many issues today of which the people are concerned. My plan in this address is to limit discussion to just four of the most prominent. My candidacy uniquely addresses each of the four as no other candidate for any US office has ever been able to do. I hope you will find the elements of my platform a welcome refreshment and inclusive of precepts that we all embrace and recognize as sincere and necessary.

My format will be to be present each issue by area of concern and then offer the specific solution which is part of my unique platform. The issues and solutions will be presented one by one in the following four topical areas:

#1—Obamacare.

#2—Illegal Immigration.

#3—Student Debt Crisis Wipe Out All Student Debt Now!

#4—Social Security's Cost-of-Living Fraud – Boost
        Social Security Now!

My pledge is to put forth legislation when elected to help address all four issues as well as full support for the platform points in Chapter 7 and the Trump agenda. Let's discuss the unique four-points above, one by one, starting with Obamacare.

Obamacare

The first problem on the list is #1 because over 54% of Americans say that the availability and affordability of healthcare is their #1 issue. Despite Obama's empty promises, many of us cannot keep our favorite doctors nor can we retain an affordable health plan that meets our needs. The costs have been so prohibitive that many Americans have forestalled doctor's visits with often grave consequences. We all know that despite what Bob Casey would offer you, Obamacare is a disaster.

My solution to Obamacare begins with clarity and definitive purpose. We start with a one-line repeal. The beast is vanquished. Following the repeal, we envision a plethora of competing less expensive alternatives provided by the marketplace without current tyrannical government controls.

Illegal Immigration

In February 2004, Arizona Senator John McCain recognized via Border Patrol reports that nearly four million people crossed our borders "illegally" each year following the Reagan amnesty in 1986. Nonetheless, the fraudulent press insists that the total count of illegal immigrants residing in the United States is eleven million, a mathematical impossibility if Border Patrol figures are to be believed. And of these millions of foreigners, countless amounts receive welfare while, contrary to popular mythology, very few actually work in agriculture.

There may be as many as 60 million and perhaps more illegal foreign nationals living in the United States today. While some individuals in this group may contribute to our society, on balance this is outweighed by the group's overall negative effect on our resources, whether they be drained by government assistance, lost employment opportunities for American citizens, or criminal offenses. It is amazing how effective the fake-ID business is in turning illegal aliens into fake citizens who are thus enabled to enjoy American rights and privileges.

According to the 2011 GAO report entitled "Criminal Alien Statistics," the cost of crimes by illegal foreign nationals is $8.1 billion per year, and that's without even considering the incomprehensibly larger emotional toll this takes on families whose priceless loved ones can never be replaced.

If elected, I will introduce two pieces of legislation that will solve this problem of illegal residents in the shadows once and for all. Besides many other benefits, it stands to save the U.S. over $1 Trillion per year in addition to major reductions in crime. The two solutions are known as pay-to-go and the resident visa program.

Pay-to-Go

It costs taxpayers $30,000 per year on the average, per illegal alien in America. Each illegal resident and their dependent children, who signs up for Pay to Go, on the way back to the home country, will receive a one-time $20,000 stipend plus the individual expense back to the home country. With a cost of $30,000 per year to support unwelcome interlopers, the taxpayer savings begins year one and continues at $30,000 per year forever. Not a bad deal for Americans.

The program therefore quietly accommodates family reunification in the home country. A family of five for example, could do quite well back home after receiving $100,000 in stipends from Uncle Sam. Reuniting families in their own countries is a good idea for them and for America. The savings in welfare means there is no cost in year one and in year 2, the savings equal $30,000 for each person who "goes." back home, never to return.

Resident Visa

Those who do not want to leave the US can sign up, be vetted, and eventually be approved for the Resident Visa. The visa will cost $200.00 to cover vetting in year one and it will be renewable every year thereafter for $100.00 To get a Resident Visa, a former interloper would agree to all stipulations after registering. Stipulations would include full initial vetting; onsite renewal vetting; keep existing jobs; new jobs for Americans first; no voting; no citizenship; no welfare and no freebies of any kind. Everybody is not automatically approved. After vetting, those not approved for the resident visa program may use the Pay-to-Go program to aid in their relocation.

As the program would entail 100% participation from illegal residents, estimates are as high as $500 billion per year cost savings in total for those who choose to go or for those who choose to stay using the no-welfare resident visa. Another $500 billion will be reclaimed over time for lost wages. Additionally, if we can figure a way for countries to reclaim their criminals, there is another $8.1 billion to be recovered.

Once the program is in effect, there would be no more illegal aliens in the country. Resident Visa holders would be legal and so there would be no shadows. There would be no need for DACA and no need for Sanctuary cities Let me repeat that. All issues with DACA would be over and Sanctuary Cities would be a thing of the past because there would be no shadows and no illegal interlopers.

Two additional programs are the part of my platform that I would now like to introduce. Like the resident alien plans, no other candidate for public office includes these great programs in their platform. You are going to love these.

These two new programs offer the promise of a positive effect on the health of the economy and both will contribute to improving it for American citizens of all ages to live well in this country. The first is about wiping out all student debt and the second is about offering Social Security recipients increased benefits to make up for fraudulent cost of living increases based on an intentionally fraudulent consumer price index.

Student Debt is Huge

If we look at the $1.48 Trillion dollars in student loan debt that more and more young adults simply cannot repay, some have asked: "Why do our young people no longer matter?" Do they matter?

We live in an age when everybody seems to have a reason to pick on millennials. They would not loan a "spoiled" millennial "ingrate" as much as a dollar for a cup of coffee.

Whether millennials are deserving of the bad rap or not, they represent a lost generation of our society. For the sake of all of America, they need to be invited back in. We all have student loan debtors in our families – sons, daughters, nephews, nieces, even grandparents and parents when we consider cosigners.

I plan to offer legislation when first elected to make sure we solve this nasty American problem. There have been many other debt reliefs in our history but none that could deliver such an immediate benefit to so many actual Americans all at once. The upside would be overwhelming, a joint humanitarian return and a major economic return far greater than any bailout in history. Let's consider.

A Bailout is a Bailout?

Many of us remember bailouts of the past from 2007 onward. We had bank bailouts, auto company bailouts, TARP bailouts and many other unnamed bailouts. Did any of these help your family? Of course not. Bailout fever began right before Obama became President and continued. The President managed all of the money—trillions. He chose not to give a dime to help student loan debt but spared no expense showering the degenerate financial institutions that owned his candidacy with gold.

Mike Collins, a Forbes Magazine contributor whose expertise focuses on manufacturing and government policy (not the former beloved magistrate of Wilkes-Barre who shares the same name) had this to say:

"Most people think that the big bank bailout was the $700 billion that the treasury department used to save the banks during the financial crash in September of 2008. But this is a long way from the truth because the bailout [ten years later] is still ongoing.

The Special Inspector General for TARP's summary of the bailout says that the total commitment of government is $16.8 trillion dollars with the $4.6 trillion already paid out. The [same] banks are now larger and still too big to fail. But it isn't just the government bailout money that tells the story of the bailout. This is a story about lies, cheating, and a multi-faceted corruption, which was often criminal."

Like most elements of his presidency, Obama made the situation worse when he commandeered the student loans from Sallie Mae and other lenders. The government now pulls in more than $50 billion a year from charging high interest rates to student borrowers. The Obama Student Loan Company charged 6.8% as a student interest rates. The CBO estimates that the interest rate on these loans could quickly be reduced from 6.8 percent to 5.3 percent if Obama had not earmarked the profit from the backs of students to subsidize Obamacare.

Not only were millennials duped into huge college loans when they were so young that Clearasil was one of their major expenses, they were duped into believing Obama was in their corner.

I believe these student victims deserve a break. They are now adults. Some stuck with huge cosign tabs are grandparents on Social security. The government actually garnishes their SSR to pay back the Obama loans.

The federal government is putting up $16.8 trillion dollars as of 2018 to big banks, and other nameless faces receiving bailouts. We still do not know who is getting our money. Yet students who are still being victimized by usury were preyed on as 17-year-olds by admissions counsellors for an all-but worthless college education leading to no job. If given the choice would you be helping the big banks or our own kids?

What do the people think about Student Debt?

Four in ten Americans believe that President Trump's administration should forgive all federal student debt in order to help stimulate the economy, according to a reasonably new survey revealed in 2017. As time goes by as more Americans realize we are excluding a full generation of Americans in our economy, this number will increase from a simple majority to an overwhelming endorsement of wiping out this scurrilous unfair debt as soon as possible. We should bring these 48 million students back into the American way of life as soon as possible.

The largest share blame for the student debt crisis lies with the promises made by over-zealous admissions counsellors convincing kids to sign up for $100,000 loans. No American can want a full generation of other Americans to be left behind in the Trump economy. We need this debt eradicated now and to install safeguards so that seventeen-year-olds in the future are never asked again to sign up for a life in debtor's prison.

According to MoneyTips.com, attitudes have changed from a time when Americans thought college students should be punished for making bad choices to today, when we could use 48 million new spenders in our economy. They would be unleashed into a world of productivity if no longer burdened with massive debt. Many of us know first-hand the consequences of this debt burden. Though millennials may not be the most gracious in asking for help, they are Americans, not DACA immigrants, and they need our help now.

The raw economic fact regardless of your philosophical preference is that spenders with the greatest potential to spend today are not spending at all in real numbers because of student debt. They are not getting married. They are not having families and they are not buying homes. We must solve this scourge on our country so that this generation can produce other generations of Americans.

Our children are not MS-13 members in disguise; there are our kids. American kids. They were snookered to join academia for what they were deceived into believing was an indispensable college degree by depraved loan sharks. Let's give them a full chance. It costs a university nothing when their students with huge loans fail. Please let that sink in.

Let me review the plight of young American college attendees and graduates. Barely out of adolescence, these young Americans were wheedled into commitments based on fraudulent promises by admissions counselors and financial institutions. It was unfair to pit experienced loan sharks against adolescent teenagers. The students were further damned by a paid-for Congress, whose lobbyists insisted that these select few with student debt, distinct from all of the others in America, had no opportunity for any relief in the bankruptcy courts.

Non-college graduates with a trillion dollars in credit card debt are still able to obtain full relief from the courts. Why did Congress exclude these former teenagers, who clearly have been the biggest victims of loan-sharking organized racketeering ever seen in America? Why?

I am pledging today to solve this problem as soon as I can. I am ready to take action. I hope you all agree. Let's help these young Americans before they are lost forever.

Young teenagers were told all through high school that the best ticket for a successful life is a college education. Is this true today? Their salaries often lag behind even those of non-college educated professionals such as plumbers, electricians, computer repair personnel, operating engineers, and more. Because of their reliance on these deliberately false misrepresentations, they now owe an approximate average of $50,000 in student debt while their admissions counsellors and loan sharks revel in riches, in their Mercedes, BMW's, and third vacation home on the lake.

Unscrupulous malefactors with self-interested agendas persuaded America's teenagers, many so young they still had Acne vulgaris, to dig themselves huge financial holes with no escape. Universities are at least partly responsible for their unfulfilled promises. Don't you think? We must also consider what liability they may share in compensating this lost generation where one out of six student borrowers must default today, a figure that only increases with time.

Removing this debt may not fully compensate for the bad hand they were dealt, but its consequent increase in economic activity will benefit all of us. It will boost the US economy beyond expectations. We are already giving bailouts of $17 billion to obscenely rich people in corporate shadows. Right now, we need a mere 10% of that to pay for the write-off of student debt without hurting taxpayers and without putting any banks under. The savings over three years, for example from the resident visa program alone pays off all the student debt that exists today. Why support illegal aliens when we can help Americans?

One last point. It helps to recall that President Obama increased the National Debt by $9.1 Trillion in just eight years, hoping to assure that illegal aliens had all the resources they needed to take as many American jobs as they could. This is six times the amount of debt owed by young Americans. Obama nearly doubled our debt. And what do we have to show for that? As is typical for the Obama years, the answer is frankly... nothing. By contrast, debt relief for our young Americans will be *visibly* positive in its impact.

So, let's say Congress wipes out all student debt because it is the fair thing to do. How do we prevent this from every happening again? For this, I thank my great friend, Dennis Grimes whose solution combines some skin in the game for Academic Institutions to the mix and thus assures that no student will ever carry debt unless the student is successful with a job in their field of study. Here is how the new loan system would work.

Nobody gets a loan unless the college or university agrees to take all of the risk of the loan. If the student is successful, she or he will pay reasonable amounts on a monthly basis. If the student is jobless, since the university vouched for the student, the school will owe all of the debt. Academic institutions are smart. They will stop lending quickly to students with very little prospects of being able to pay the loan back. If students do not maintain acceptable averages, they will be expelled, and the university will pay their balance. If they want to go to college in the future, it will be cash only. What do you think?

A Rigged System

I am confident that President Trump would re-enfranchising America's youngest generation of adults by eradicating student debt and pay the balance via savings no longer spent subsidizing illegal immigrants.

In his own words, regarding recent graduates: "They go, and they work, and they take loans, and they're borrowed up, and they can't breathe, and they get through college and the worst thing is, they go through that whole process and they don't have any job." Trump has it right. He sees how this rigged system has snuffed out the optimism of a bright generation that now gives way to cynicism and despair.

If I am elected as your Senator, I will help enact legislation that eradicates all Student Debt, effective immediately.

Boost Social Security Now

Social Security is no longer publicly discussed by our duplicitous media despite the fact that seniors' issues need the spotlight now more than ever. The media derided the implied greed of SSR recipients who received a whopping two percent cost of living raise to kick off 2018, as if oblivious to the fact that the inflation rate for 2017 was nearly 11%. Not 2%, but 11%.

No wonder seniors are struggling when their cost for purchases goes up 11% and their COLA to make up for that is a mere 2%. How do I know that, and you don't?

There are several ways Americans can investigate how much government lies cost them each year. The government purposely underestimates the cost of living to deprive our elderly of a commensurate actual increase in earned benefits. One such method for you to use is to subscribe to the Chapwood index or you may explore Shadowstats.com.

Seniors unfortunately are running out of whatever financial cushions they may ever have had, and their plight today is dire. I encourage you all to research the degree to which government deceptions are resulting in these surreptitious deprivations.

After decades being saturated by our mainstream propaganda rags, it is refreshing to finally see the truth in print. The Chapwood Index reflects the true cost-of-living increase in America. It is updated and released twice a year. There the ruses or mis-directions of the government are not included in its pages. Instead, it truthfully reports the unadjusted actual cost and price fluctuation of the top 500 items on which Americans spend their after-tax dollars in the 50 largest cities in the nation.

It exposes why middle-class Americans—salaried workers who are given routine pay hikes and retirees who depend on annual increases in their corporate pension and Social Security payments—cannot maintain their standard of living. Plainly and simply, the Index shows that their income can't keep up with their expenses and it explains why they increasingly have to turn to the government for entitlements for supplementation.

Mainstream Democrats like Senator Casey and Nancy Pelosi exacerbate the situation by allowing use of even more inequitable methods such as the new chained CPI to help assure that Seniors can languish in poverty as soon as possible.

The problem of lacking transparency on true costs (true inflation) occurs because salary and benefit increases are pegged to the fraudulent Consumer Price Index (CPI), which for more than a century has purported to reflect the fluctuation in prices for a typical "basket of goods" in American cities — but which actually hasn't done that for more than 30 years

The middle class has seen its purchasing power decline dramatically in the last three decades, forcing more and more people to seek entitlements when their savings are gone. And as long as pay raises and benefit increases are tied to a false CPI, this trend will continue.

In the past, nobody was anxious to throw the proverbial grandma under the bus. Now, believe it or not, hordes of constituencies are lining up to be the first to fleece what should belong to her into the eternal abyss, never to be seen again. The list of offenders includes: Congress, government officials, professors in academia, the "greatest" economic advisors the world has ever known, and dejected stand-alone economists who failed to gain tenure at a university.

This group of elite misfits have formed a diabolical consortium to cheat seniors out of their due cost of living increases promised from the very day the SSR act was passed by Franklin Delano Roosevelt.

As the mainstream Democrats kowtow to cultural elites and financial institutions, turning their backs on the workers and middle-class that defined their constituency for much of the 20th century, it is up to us to pick up the slack and fight for the rights of everyday Americans. When SSR was enacted, the president promised full dollar value throughout the years in order to ensure its passage in 1933. We cannot let this be undermined by the likes of Senator Casey and his allies under Chuck Schumer and Nancy Pelosi.

Many Americans are concerned that the Social Security program itself may not be able to sustain itself while others see the government cheating on the cost of living increases (CPI) thereby predetermining a life of squalor for seniors.

All successful societies throughout the ages, have maintained respect and dignity for their elders. Not only is cheating seniors a moral failure, it is a sign of a civilization entering an era of decay.

While seniors are losing their homes and many, for want of bread and milk, are on the verge of heading to the proverbial poorhouse or worse—the clutches of the Grim Reaper, Congress in 2018 pretended to care, giving a 2% raise, but then quickly snatched it right back in the dead of night via a Medicare Part B premium increase. This additional Medicare Part B charge for necessary health services for seniors was excluded from the cost of living calculations.

Thus, to pay Medicare part B, seniors are forced to use their "generous" 2% raises there, rather than to offset the costs brought forth from inflation in 2017 for which the 2% was intended. Since the real inflationary cost increases were closer to 11%, that means that instead of 9% that seniors were to endure, they accrued a full load of 11% in price increases. It's easy to understand why this constant drainage of resources is unsustainable for a senior citizen.

How did we reach this point?

Early in the administration of disgraced former President Bill Clinton, an economist named Michael Boskin, and Alan Greenspan, Chairman of the Board of Governors of the Federal Reserve System, devised a scheme that would allow for market basket "substitutions" to artificially lower the cost of living and result in lower payments to our oldest Americans. Prior to their involvement, the consumer price index (CPI) was measured using the cost of a fixed basket of goods, a fairly simple and straightforward concept.

The identical basket of goods would be priced at prevailing market costs for each period, and the period-to-period change in the cost of that market basket represented the rate of inflation in terms of maintaining a constant standard of living. That was self-evidently fair and reasonable, and predictably resulted in seniors receiving annual COLA increases in tandem with the prices of goods actually increasing.

But Boskin and Alan Greenspan argued that when one item in the basket, for instance steak, became too expensive, the consumer would substitute hamburger for the steak, and that the inflation measure should reflect the costs tied to buying hamburger rather than the steak. Eventually, it became OK for the bureaucrats to replace hamburger with less expensive tuna and eventually because the protein value was the same, cat tuna replaced regular tuna in the market basket.

To further obscure the true cost of living, other items were selectively removed from the basket when the prices were high and then reinserted when the prices were low.

Many people have been familiar with this ruse. For example, a 1970s economic commentator named Barry Ritholtz joked that Greenspan's core inflation metric can more accurately be described as "inflation ex-inflation," meaning inflation after all of the inflation has been excluded. This demonstrates that the deception of seniors has been intentional, and it continues with a new notion called the chained CPI that will cost seniors even more.

The fact is that government has deceitfully stolen right from the pockets of our beloved seniors by denying them a fair cost of living increase. Some have even suggested that the government believes a natural limit exists on the criticism this could engender because over time, many of the complaints will be silenced by their deaths. Charming.

Walter J. Williams, an American blessing who operates the Shadowstats site has demonstrated that seniors have been stiffed by much more than just 125% and in fact should be receiving more than 4 times what their dollars were worth in 1980. That's $450 instead of $100.00. Any senior would love to have even a small proportion of that loss back.

I hope I have convinced you all that seniors have been ripped off and are being ripped off financially by their government. Congress is the real culprit.

So, what do I recommend for now? A gradual remedy. Since it would be difficult to give seniors the proper increase immediately needed to offset this quagmire caused by government malfeasance, my recommendation would be to approach it gradually, in a way that seniors would be somewhat pleased, and be able to live out their golden years in a more dignified manner.

For the next four years, the COLA boost that I'd recommend would be 15% above the real inflation rate. After four consecutive years, that should be sufficient to remove seniors from the on-deck circle they currently occupy directly outside the homeless shelter. That's all it would take.

Thank you for your attention on these important matters.

In conclusion, I must again express my gratitude for your consideration and any support as we work together to make America even greater.

God bless America and help us all make her better

Other books by Brian Kelly: (amazon.com, and Kindle)

It's Time for The John Doe Party… Don't you think? By By Elephants.
Great Players in Florida Gators Football… Tim Tebow and a ton of other great players
Great Coaches in Florida Gators Football… The best coaches in Gator history.
The Constitution by Hamilton, Jefferson, Madison, et al. The Real Constitution
The Constitution Companion. Will help you learn and understand the Constitution
Great Coaches in Clemson Football The best Clemson Coaches right to Dabo Sinney
Great Players in Clemson Football The best Clemson players in history
Winning Back America. America's been stolen and can be won back completely
The Founding of America… Great book to pick up a lot of great facts
Defeating America's Career Politicians. The scoundrels need to go.
Midnight Mass by Jack Lammers… You remember what it was like Hreat story
The Bike by Jack Lammers… Great heartwarming Story by Jack
Wipe Out All Student Loan Debt--Now! Watch the economy go boom!
No Free Lunch Pay Back Welfare! Why not pay it back?
Deport All Millennials Now!!! Why they deserve to be deported and/or saved
DELETE the EPA, Please! The worst decisions to hurt America
Taxation Without Representation 4th Edition Should we throw the TEA overboard again?
Four Great Political Essays by Thomas Dawson
Top Ten Political Books for 2018… Cliffnotes Version of 10 Political Books
Top Six Patriotic Books for 2018… Cliffnotes version of 6 Patriotic Boosk
Why Trump Got Elected!.. It's great to hear about a great milestone in America!
The Day the Free Press Died. Corrupt Press Lives on!
Solved (Immigration) The best solutions for 2018
Solved II (Obamacare, Social Security, Student Debt) Check it out; They're solved.
Great Moments in Pittsburgh Steelers Football... Six Super Bowls and more.
Great Players in Pittsburgh Steelers Football ,,,Chuck Noll, Bill Cowher, Mike Tomin, etc.
Great Coaches in New England Patriots Football,,, Bill Belichick the one and only plus others
Great Players in New England Patriots Football… Tom Brady, Drew Bledsoe et al.
Great Coaches in Philadelphia Eagles Football..Andy Reid, Doug Pederson & Lots more
Great Players in Philadelphia Eagles Football Great players such as Sonny Jurgenson
Great Coaches in Syracuse Football All the greats including Ben Schwartzwalder
Great Players in Syracuse Football. Highlights best players such as Jim Brown & Donovan McNabb
Millennials are People Too !!! Give US millennials help to live American Dream
Brian Kelly for the United States Senate from PA: Fresh Face for US Senate
The Candidate's Bible. Don't pray for your campaign without this bible
Rush Limbaugh's Platform for Americans… Rush will love it
Sean Hannity's Platform for Americans… Sean will love it
Donald Trump's New Platform for Americans. Make Trump unbeatable in 2020
Tariffs Are Good for America! One of the best tools a president can have
Great Coaches in Pittsburgh Steelers Football Sixteen of the best coaches ever to coach in pro football.
Great Moments in New England Patriots Football Great football moments from Boston to New England
Great Moments in Philadelphia Eagles Football. The best from the Eagles from the beginning of football.
Great Moments in Syracuse Football The great moments, coaches & players in Syracuse Football
Boost Social Security Now! Hey Buddy Can You Spare a Dime?
The Birth of American Football. From the first college game in 1869 to the last Super Bowl
Obamacare: A One-Line Repeal Congress must get this done.
A Wilkes-Barre Christmas Story A wonderful town makes Christmas all the better
A Boy, A Bike, A Train, and a Christmas Miracle A Christmas story that will melt your heart
Pay-to-Go   America-First Immigration Fix
Legalizing Illegal Aliens Via Resident Visas Americans-first plan saves $Trillions. Learn how!
60 Million Illegal Aliens in America!!! A simple, America-first solution.
The Bill of Rights By Founder James Madison Refresh your knowledge of the specific rights for all
Great Players in Army Football Great Army Football played by great players..
Great Coaches in Army Football Army's coaches are all great.
Great Moments in Army Football Army Football at its best.
Great Moments in Florida Gators Football Gators Football from the start. This is the book.
Great Moments in Clemson Football CU Football at its best. This is the book.
Great Moments in Florida Gators Football Gators Football from the start. This is the book.
The Constitution Companion. A Guide to Reading and Comprehending the Constitution
The Constitution by Hamilton, Jefferson, & Madison – Big type and in English
PATERNO: The Dark Days After Win # 409. Sky began to fall within days of win # 409.

JoePa 409 Victories: Say No More! Winningest Division I-A football coach ever
American College Football: The Beginning From before day one football was played.
Great Coaches in Alabama Football Challenging the coaches of every other program!
Great Coaches in Penn State Football the Best Coaches in PSU's football program
Great Players in Penn State Football The best players in PSU's football program
Great Players in Notre Dame Football The best players in ND's football program
Great Coaches in Notre Dame Football The best coaches in any football program
Great Players in Alabama Football from Quarterbacks to offensive Linemen Greats!
Great Moments in Alabama Football AU Football from the start. This is the book.
Great Moments in Penn State Football PSU Football, start--games, coaches, players,
Great Moments in Notre Dame Football ND Football, start, games, coaches, players
Cross Country with the Parents A great trip from East Coast to West with the kids
Seniors, Social Security & the Minimum Wage. Things seniors need to know.
How to Write Your First Book and Publish It with CreateSpace
The US Immigration Fix--It's all in here. Finally, an answer.
I had a Dream IBM Could be #1 Again The title is self-explanatory
WineDiets.Com Presents The Wine Diet Learn how to lose weight while having fun.
Wilkes-Barre, PA; Return to Glory Wilkes-Barre City's return to glory
Geoffrey Parsons' Epoch... The Land of Fair Play Better than the original.
The Bill of Rights 4 Dummmies! This is the best book to learn about your rights.
Sol Bloom's Epoch …Story of the Constitution The best book to learn the Constitution
America 4 Dummmies! All Americans should read to learn about this great country.
The Electoral College 4 Dummmies! How does it really work?
The All-Everything Machine Story about IBM's finest computer server.
ThankYou IBM! This book explains how IBM was beaten in the computer marketplace by neophytes

Brian has written 171 books in total. Other books can be found at amazon.com/author/brianwkell